Alcoholism

Titles in the Diseases and Disorders series include:

DISEASES & DISORDERS

Alcoholism

Sheila Wyborny

LUCENT BOOKS
A part of Gale, Cengage Learning

GALE
CENGAGE Learning

Detroit • New York • San Francisco • New Haven, Conn • Waterville, Maine • London

LIBRARY OF CONGRESS CATALOGING-IN-PUBLICATION DATA

Wyborny, Sheila, 1950-
  Alcoholism / by Sheila Wyborny.
    p. cm. — (Diseases and disorders)
  Includes bibliographical references and index.
  ISBN-13: 978-1-59018-996-2 (hardcover)
  1. Alcoholism—Juvenile literature. I. Title.
  RC565.W93 2008
  616.86'1—dc22

                                                    2007032093

ISBN-10: 1-59018-996-5

Printed in the United States of America
  3 4 5 6 7 12 11 10 09 08

Table of Contents

"The Most Difficult Puzzles Ever Devised"

Charles Best, one of the pioneers in the search for a cure for diabetes, once explained what it is about medical research that intrigued him so. "It's not just the gratification of knowing one is helping people," he confided, "although that probably is a more heroic and selfless motivation. Those feelings may enter in, but truly, what I find best is the feeling of going toe to toe with nature, of trying to solve the most difficult puzzles ever devised. The answers are there somewhere, those keys that will solve the puzzle and make the patient well. But how will those keys be found?"

Since the dawn of civilization, nothing has so puzzled people—and often frightened them, as well—as the onset of illness in a body or mind that had seemed healthy before. A seizure, the inability of a heart to pump, the sudden deterioration of muscle tone in a small child—being unable to reverse such conditions or even to understand why they occur was unspeakably frustrating to healers. Even before there were names for such conditions, even before they were understood at all, each

6

was a reminder of how complex the human body was, and how vulnerable.

While our grappling with understanding diseases has been frustrating at times, it has also provided some of humankind's most heroic accomplishments. Alexander Fleming's accidental discovery in 1928 of a mold that could be turned into penicillin has resulted in the saving of untold millions of lives. The isolation of the enzyme insulin has reversed what was once a death sentence for anyone with diabetes. There have been great strides in combating conditions for which there is not yet a cure, too. Medicines can help AIDS patients live longer, diagnostic tools such as mammography and ultrasounds can help doctors find tumors while they are treatable, and laser surgery techniques have made the most intricate, minute operations routine.

This "toe-to-toe" competition with diseases and disorders is even more remarkable when seen in a historical continuum. An astonishing amount of progress has been made in a very short time. Just two hundred years ago, the existence of germs as a cause of some diseases was unknown. In fact, it was less than 150 years ago that a British surgeon named Joseph Lister had difficulty persuading his fellow doctors that washing their hands before delivering a baby might increase the chances of a healthy delivery (especially if they had just attended to a diseased patient)!

Each book in Lucent's Diseases and Disorders series explores a disease or disorder and the knowledge that has been accumulated (or discarded) by doctors through the years. Each book also examines the tools used for pinpointing a diagnosis, as well as the various means that are used to treat or cure a disease. Finally, new ideas are presented—techniques or medicines that may be on the horizon.

Frustration and disappointment are still part of medicine, for not every disease or condition can be cured or prevented. But the limitations of knowledge are being pushed outward constantly; the "most difficult puzzles ever devised" are finding challengers every day.

Alcoholism: Compulsive Behavior or Disease?

Just the word "alcoholism" has the power to evoke a wide variety of responses. For the adult child of an alcoholic parent, the word may trigger memories of a childhood lived in constant fear of physical abuse, isolation, or having to take on adult responsibilities at far too early an age. A more distant relative of an alcoholic may recall an aunt or uncle displaying erratic, or strange, behavior after consuming too much alcohol at a family gathering. For those who have never dealt with alcoholism on a personal level, it is an abstract concept that is someone else's problem. Someone who has lost a loved one in a drunk driving accident, however, understands all too well that alcoholism and alcohol abuse can have devastating results for anyone, including nondrinkers. In addition to the different ways people respond to alcoholism and alcoholics, a number of scientists, therapists, and physicians disagree as to what alcoholism actually is.

A Compulsive Behavior

Just as people react differently to the subject of alcoholism, the very definition of the term also varies. Some psychiatrists and other therapists believe alcoholism is a compulsive behavior, with emphasis on behavior, rather than mental disorder. They suggest that correcting the problem is a matter of learning to make healthful decisions and of taking control:

> Many types of compulsive behavior, including alcoholism, are incorrectly viewed as diseases. Alcoholism was originally termed a disease in order to help people understand that it is a serious problem for which they should seek help. However, the disease model has been overused and distorted to the extent that many alcoholics and other emotionally disturbed people incorrectly believe that

Adult children of alcoholics remember the pain of emotional and physical abuse suffered while growing up.

Some therapists believe that alcoholism is a compulsive behavior rather than a disease.

they are physically "sick" and need medical rather than psychological help to overcome their addictions.[1]

Researchers who define alcoholism as a form of compulsive behavior believe that to categorize it as a disease encourages alcoholics to give up the responsibility for their own lives and choices and to perceive themselves as victims. When viewed as a disease, the alcoholism is not of their own making and they need someone else to "cure" it. They will use anything from stressful incidents, such as problems at work, to boredom as an excuse to drink. Professionals who agree with the alcoholism-as-a-compulsive-behavior model believe that treating alcoholism as a disease is harmful to the long-term dignity and self-esteem of alcoholics. According to these professionals, some alcoholics use illness to excuse their behavior and use their perceived illness as a tool to manipulate their friends and family. For instance, some alcoholics coerce wives, husbands, or children to call in sick to their employers for them, when, in fact, the alcoholic may be on a drinking binge or not feel well in the aftermath of a drinking binge.

In contrast, according to the alcoholism-as-a-compulsive-behavior model, people can accept responsibility for excessive drinking and control their own behavior. Additionally, if alcoholism were labeled a behavior and not a disease, the $7-billion-a-year treatment and rehabilitation industry might suffer. This is because insurance policies that cover only problems defined as physical illness or injury would not cover counseling for alcoholism.

A Disease

A wider and more publicly recognized belief is that alcoholism, also known as alcohol dependence, is a disease, or a bodily ailment. If alcoholism is a disease, then alcoholics have little or no control over their drinking habits. Some scientists even believe an alcoholic's body works differently from the body of someone who is not an alcoholic. They believe an alcoholic's metabolism functions at a different rate than that of non-alcoholics and that genetics play a key role in alcoholism. According to this model, environment is also a major factor in alcoholism. For instance, children whose adult family members drink excessively may accept this as normal adult behavior. In fact, some studies have shown that children of alcoholics are three to four times more likely to become alcoholics themselves than children of nonalcoholics.

According to the American Medical Association, alcoholism is a chronic, progressive disease that appears to be genetic because it can usually be traced down a family tree:

It starts innocently with a couple of drinks, but they affect people very differently. Some feel fuzzy and removed but others experience almost a state of euphoria. Those who get a rush appear to be predisposed to alcoholism, a disease that can have devastating physical, spiritual, psychological, emotional, and occupational consequences.[2]

Experts also disagree over how to confront and treat alcoholism. Some groups, like Alcoholics Anonymous (AA), function from the standpoint that alcoholics have no control over regulating their drinking. The group believes that the only way to successfully treat alcoholism is through total abstinence—to consume no alcohol at all. AA members also believe alcoholism cannot be cured, and that since there is no cure, there are no former alcoholics, only recovering ones. Other groups, however, believe people with alcohol dependency can be trained to take control of their drinking rather than abstain from it. They can learn to taper off their alcohol consumption and stop after one or two drinks.

Whether the alcoholic practices total abstinence or limits alcohol consumption, though, there is always the risk that using alcohol will put the person into a self-destructive cycle. People who drink too much become inebriated and lose control of their bodies and their judgment. This is dangerous behavior whether a person is an alcoholic or not. Some people who occasionally drink too much are not alcoholics; they are simply behaving irresponsibly. However, if drinking too much becomes a habit, even the occasional drinker can become an alcoholic.

Symptoms of Alcoholism

Symptoms of alcoholism include unstable, sometimes erratic emotional behavior or violent outbursts; the inability to limit alcohol consumption; blackouts; a strong need or compulsion to drink, regardless of consequences; and the ability to consume large quantities of alcohol before exhibiting any behaviors connected with drunkenness. The alcoholic may also suffer from physical symptoms such as abdominal pain, nausea, blurred vision, or vomiting. These are not only symptoms of alcoholics but also of people who occasionally drink too much. Physical symptoms can vary from person to person.

Whether alcoholism is a disease or a compulsive behavior, no one denies that it is a major health problem in many countries and cultures throughout the world. Most people would also agree that alcoholism is devastating to alcoholics and to those who care about them. Alcoholism can cost people their self-respect, their careers, families, friends, health, and even their own lives. Alcoholism is often chronic and progressive. For instance, in its earliest stages, the need for only one or two drinks in order to relax can escalate over time to needing eight or ten drinks to produce the same effect. Despite all that is known about alcoholism and the efforts that have been made to educate the public, some old attitudes persist. At times, alcoholism is hidden, excused, ridiculed, or denied. It is glossed over with little more than a wink and a nod and considered a socially acceptable, or at least socially tolerated, form of addiction.

CHAPTER ONE

How Serious a Problem is Alcoholism?

Alcoholism has been a serious health and social problem in America for many years. However, Americans have not always recognized alcoholism as a form of drug abuse. Over the years, alcoholism has frequently been portrayed in movies and on television as amusing behavior. For example, alcoholics have been characterized as the small-town drunk who locks himself up in the jail cell after a Saturday night bender; the neighborhood bar patron who has trouble finding his hat on his head after having several drinks too many; and the likable uncle who drinks too much at the family holiday dinner, puts his coat on backwards, trips over his own feet as he heads out the door, and stabs his key at the ignition several times before he starts his car and weaves his way home, glancing off the curbs like a billiard ball.

Portrayals such as these can mask the true nature of alcoholism and the grave consequences that can result from alcohol abuse or alcohol dependence. Alcohol is, in fact, a drug. People can become addicted to alcohol as they can to any other

Amusing portrayals of drunks, like Lee Marvin (and his horse) in
Cat Ballou, mask the seriousness of problem drinking.

drug. The seriousness of alcohol abuse in the United States was
clearly described in 1997 by then–drug czar Barry McCaffrey,
director of the Office of National Drug Control Policy (ONDCP),
who said, "Undoubtedly, alcohol is the principal drug use problem in America today."[3]

Despite this knowledge, many people continue to look upon alcoholism and alcohol abuse, in general, in a more tolerant way than other forms of drug abuse. One reason is that alcohol can be legally purchased by adults, that is, anyone over age 21. It is familiar, accessible, and relatively inexpensive. For these reasons, alcohol can appear nonthreatening rather than as a substance that can lead to addiction, dangerous behavior, and other serious problems.

During Prohibition, when it was illegal to sell or even drink alcohol, people found alcohol at secret clubs called speakeasies.

Several famous authors, including Ernest Hemingway, were known alcoholics.

A Brief History of Socially Acceptable Addiction

Prohibition was a period of time in the United States when the manufacture, marketing, or transportation of liquor, or alcohol, in this country or in any of its territories was illegal. Prohibition became law with the 18th Amendment, also called the Dry Law, on January 16, 1920. This law remained in effect until it was repealed by the 21st Amendment on December 5, 1933. The law was first passed because people blamed alcohol abuse for much of the crime and violence in America. Many people did not agree with the law, however, and found ways to

Alcoholism provided material for such comedians as W.C. Fields.

purchase alcohol illegally at places such as speakeasies. These were clubs that had locked doors and could only be entered by invitation or password. At speakeasies, alcohol was often served in teacups.

When Prohibition ended, the speakeasies closed and drinking came back out into the open. It was glamorized in movies as a sophisticated social pastime with popular movie stars shown dressed in the height of fashion, drinking from fine crystal. The "three-martini lunch" was a popular phrase. Successful businessmen were known to make important deals while drinking their lunch. Additionally, several of America's most popular authors, including William Faulkner, Eugene O'Neill, and Ernest Hemingway, were known alcoholics. Hemingway is credited with a number of quotes concerning alcohol. Some of his statements provide significant insight into the thought processes of an alcoholic. He wrote, "It was as natural as eating and to me as necessary, and I would not have thought of eating a meal without drinking a beer."[4]

Hemingway is also credited with a remark in which he seems to offer one excuse for getting drunk: "An intelligent man is sometimes forced to be drunk to spend time with his fools."[5]

If average people were to believe what they saw on the movie screen and read in magazines and books, handsome actors, beautiful actresses, and famous authors drank alcohol, so many people felt if they drank they were in good company. Alcoholism also provided material for the comedians of the

In the 1970s, a group of entertainers known as the Rat Pack (including Dean Martin, Sammy Davis Jr., and Frank Sinatra, shown here) gave the message that being drunk is fun.

Hatchet Carrie

Carrie Nation was a leading figure in the temperance (abstinence in the use of alcohol) movement. Born Carrie Moore in 1846, she grew to the formidable size of nearly 6 feet and weighed 175 pounds. She acquired the last name Nation when she married her second husband, Dr. David Nation, a physician nineteen years her senior. Nation gained her fame by entering Kansas saloons and smashing their liquor stocks with large rocks, which she called smashers.

Soon, though, Nation and her hymn-singing followers graduated to using hatchets to wreak havoc on saloonkeepers. She was frequently arrested, but the law did not slow her in her mission. She paid her fines from the speaking fees she earned and the sale of souvenir hatchets. Nation collapsed while making one of her speeches in Eureka Springs, Arkansas, and died on June 9, 1911.

Carrie Nation was a formidable leading figure in the temperance movement.

Pretty, sweet alcoholic drinks can lead people to drink more than they should.

day. Comedian W.C. Fields once said, "I always keep a bottle of whisky handy . . . in case I see a snake, which I also keep handy."[6] Similarly, Joe E. Lewis also got his share of laughs making jokes about alcoholism. He once said, "I distrust camels and anyone else who can go a week without a drink."[7] One of Lewis's one-liners, however, may describe the behavior of many alcoholics: "I drink to forget I drink."[8]

In some homes, drunken guests were the norm. If a person attending a party had a reputation as a heavy drinker, more responsible hosts might tuck the guest into a bedroom to

Blind Pigs and Speakeasies

Blind pigs and speakeasies were private clubs where alcoholic beverages were illegally sold and consumed. Usually owned and operated by organized crime groups, these illegal business enterprises sprang up throughout the country in huge numbers during the Prohibition era of the 1920s and 1930s. For instance, at one time, there were believed to be about one hundred thousand of these enterprises in New York City alone. In fact, the small area of the city along 52nd Street between Fifth and Sixth Avenues had the reputation of having the highest concentration of liquor-selling establishments anywhere in the country.

It was expensive for these club owners to stay in business, though. They had to go to great lengths to keep from being shut down. For one thing, patrons had to knock for entrance and supply the doorman with a password or phrase, which was frequently changed. Additionally, they had to pay off local federal agents, police, and members of other agencies who were willing to accept bribes and look the other way. To protect themselves from honest law enforcement personnel, owners installed elaborate alarm systems and secret hiding places for their liquor supplies. They also hired their own security people to be on the lookout for law enforcement raiding teams. When Prohibition ended, there was no more need for these secret clubs. Many closed, but some went legitimate and operated for the most part within the boundaries of the law.

Blind pigs and speakeasies were private clubs where alcohol was illegally sold during Prohibition.

sleep off the effects or send the guest home in a taxi. Other hosts, however, would turn a blind eye, allowing the inebriated guest to drive himself home. At this time, drunk drivers were not treated as criminals, unless they were involved in serious accidents. If the drunk driver was a famous actor or important politician, the public often did not hear about it.

Even as recently as the 1970s excessive drinking was portrayed in movies and on television as little more than a recreational activity. A group of entertainers, collectively known as the Rat Pack, frequently appeared on stage and in the movies, with drinks in hand, stumbling up steps and slurring their speech. Whether the behavior was from alcohol or playacting, the message was the same. Being drunk is fun and makes a person more popular. Alcohol is a party in a bottle.

Even though public attitude and laws governing the abuse of alcohol have changed in recent years to reflect the seriousness of alcoholism, drinking is still a popular social pastime. Many adults today get together for drinks in restaurants, bars, and clubs, or gather in friends' homes for drinks. Having a drink or two after work is sometimes called unwinding and is a way to relax after a challenging and stressful day. When people begin to use this excuse to drink on a daily basis, though, they could be developing a serious problem.

Few people who view themselves as social drinkers like the taste of straight alcohol. However, over the years, many sweet and attractive drinks have been developed to disguise the taste of alcohol. Ginger ale, fruit juices, even flavored gelatins are added to make the flavor of alcohol more appealing. Alcohol can be served "on the rocks" (with ice), or whipped in a blender with crushed ice into a drink with a consistency similar to that of a snow cone. Alcoholic drinks may be served with olives or tiny onions, decorated with colorful swizzle sticks or tiny paper umbrellas, or served in specially designed plastic cups as the signature drinks of popular bars. All of this dressing up of drinks can make alcohol appear attractive, fun, and nonthreatening. However, adding sweet flavors and other disguises to drinks leads some people to consume excessive amounts of alcohol, drinking until their judgment is impaired and their health and safety are compromised.

Advertising and Alcoholism

In addition to being made into pretty drinks, alcohol is made attractive in other ways. Alcohol and alcohol advertising are big business. For instance, in 2006, 703 million gallons of domestic and foreign wine were sold in the United States. Beer sales average about 6.2 billion gallons annually. Alcohol-related businesses employ over three million people and pay more than twenty billion dollars in taxes every year, contributing over $50

Advertising strives to link drinking alcohol to something that is attractive or fun.

billion to America's economy. In 2002, the United States alcohol industry spent nearly $2 billion on ads for magazines and newspapers, radio, television, and billboards.

Alcohol companies have huge advertising budgets at their disposal because the production of alcohol is such a large industry. They spend huge sums of money on market research to determine the best ways to sell more of their products to specific groups of people. Billboards, newspaper and magazine ads, and television and radio commercials are geared toward specific demographic groups. Some of this advertising is designed to appeal to women, some to men, and some are created specifically to attract the attention of people of certain age groups.

Alcohol companies continually work to develop ways to make their products more attractive, accessible, and affordable to a wider range of customers. For instance, more liquor stores have opened in strip malls near neighborhoods. Bars and liquor stores are open longer hours, and some alcohol products are very inexpensive. People have the option of drinking too much for very little money. Patricia Taylor, a director with the Center for Science in the Public Interest, commenting on the trend toward producing cheap alcoholic beverages, said, "In many areas, it is possible to buy a 6-pack of beer for less [money] than a 6-pack of some brand-name soft drinks."[9]

Both commercials and ads strive to link drinking to something that is attractive or entertaining. They show drinking as fun, that it is an important element in having a good time, and that drinking alcohol is sexy. Some people get the idea from advertising that drinking alcohol will help them gain acceptance in popular groups, improve their self-esteem, or make them more attractive to the opposite sex. This is because only attractive people appear in the ads and on the commercials. The actors are always well-groomed, slender, and often engaged in activities that require good physical coordination. Advertisers never depict drinkers as overweight, uncoordinated, bleary-eyed, or unkempt.

In advertising, drinking, particularly beer drinking, is heavily linked with sports, sporting events, and athletes. For instance, in 2002, alcohol producers devoted 60 percent of their $991 million television advertising budget to sports programming.

In addition to radio and television commercials during sporting events, alcohol advertising appears inside many professional sports stadiums in the form of large posters and billboards. Many of these sports stadiums feature ads for alcohol on walls facing the playing fields and on scoreboards.

Some stadiums are named for alcohol companies. According to some reports, in 1995, Coors Brewing Company of Golden, Colorado, paid $15 million for naming rights to Coors Field, in Denver, Colorado, hometown of the Colorado Rockies baseball team. Many professional sports stadiums also host major events for high school and college teams. This results in high school and college students being exposed to this advertising during their events as well.

Alcohol advertising is often linked to sports and appears in or near sports stadiums.

Some stadiums, like Coors Field, are named for alcohol companies.

In addition to all of the advertising alcohol companies do on television and radio in connection with professional sporting events, vendors sell alcohol products during games. This often leads to out-of-control behavior of fans. In some stadiums, the management does not have enough law enforcement people on hand during professional games to monitor the behavior of drunken fans. In fact, the Harvard School of Public Health College Alcohol Study of 2002 concluded that many sports fans drink heavily at sporting events. Alcohol vendors inside sports stadiums as well as pre- and post-game tailgate parties outside the stadiums in parking lots ensure the free and heavy flow of alcohol as people come out to support their favorite teams.

The alcohol industry has close ties with nearly every professional sports association including the National Football League (NFL), the National Basketball Association, Major League Baseball, the National Hockey League, professional soccer, and the National Association for Stock Car Auto Racing. Some of these groups have policies, at least on paper, to limit alcohol consumption at professional events. The NFL, for example, has a policy limiting the number of beers served at one time to each customer during a professional game and requiring that alcohol sales end by the fourth quarter of the game. However, investigative reports, such as CBS's *Inside Edition* have proven that some alcohol vendors either choose to ignore these limits or are unable to enforce them due to the sheer number of customers they serve during games.

Some people argue that alcohol advertising does not increase the use or abuse of alcohol. For instance, results of a University of Texas study of alcohol advertising covering a period of twenty-one years indicate that the amount of money alcohol companies spend on advertising has no significant relationship to total alcohol consumption. Some also contend that alcohol is a product for mature people who already know what excessive alcohol consumption can cause and so are not affected by alcohol brand name advertising. According to studies sponsored by the alcohol industry, more alcohol consumption is shown during television programs than on television commercials for alcohol. They further argue that the more frequently alcohol appears on television the more it is identified with more commonplace products like cookies and aspirin. They say this reduces the likelihood of nondrinkers beginning to use alcohol or drinkers to abuse it. However, groups who support alcohol advertising concede that alcohol is portrayed in a favorable way in alcohol commercials and ads by showing it being consumed by attractive people.

Popular Myths That Can Contribute to Alcoholism

One way to discourage behavior that leads to alcoholism is to separate fact from fiction. There are dozens of popular myths about beer alone. For instance, some people believe beer is not as harmful or addictive as liquor because beer does not contain as much alcohol as whiskey and other hard liquor. Because of this belief, people think they can drink more beers than mixed drinks without getting drunk. This myth can have serious consequences. One 12-ounce can of beer contains just as much

A popular myth about beer is that it is not as harmful or addictive as liquor.

alcohol as a glass of wine, an average mixed drink, or a cocktail; therefore, three or four cans of beer are as intoxicating as three or four mixed drinks. Some people believe light-colored beer has less alcohol than dark-colored beer. This is not true. Beer color comes from the toasted malts. This affects color but has nothing to do with alcohol content. It is also not true that American beer contains less alcohol than European beer. A final myth about beer is that people who drink only beer will not become alcoholics. The fact is, beer contains alcohol, alco-

Another myth is that eating a big meal before drinking will keep a person sober.

hol is a drug, and drugs are addictive. Heavy beer drinkers are just as likely to become alcoholics as people who overindulge in other types of alcohol.

Another myth is that mixing types of alcohol, called mixing the grain and the grape, will make a person more intoxicated than sticking with one type of alcohol. Alcohol is alcohol. While mixing types of drinks may cause an upset stomach, a person cannot hope to remain sober drinking, say, five glasses of wine instead of three beers and two glasses of wine.

When people drink too much and become intoxicated, though, they sometimes try a variety of strategies to rid their bodies of the symptoms of excessive drinking. Taking cold showers, walking in fresh air, or drinking several cups of hot coffee are popularly believed to speed the return to sobriety. These methods simply do not work. There are no quick fixes for getting sober. The only cure is time, at a rate of about one hour per ounce of alcohol consumed. This is the time it takes the liver to detoxify the body. Accordingly, if a person has five drinks, the body will not be rid of the symptoms for five hours.

One old saying goes, "Give a drunk a cup of coffee and all you have is a wide-awake drunk."

Any attempt to try to rush the effects of alcohol from the body can have tragic results. A cold shower or a few cups of coffee might make a person feel more wide awake, but the body is still impaired by the effects of alcohol. Attempting to rush sobriety with coffee or cold showers will not return the body's reflexes to normal or enable a person to make responsible choices. Drunk driving, with or without coffee, is illegal and dangerous. It is best to allow the person to sleep or rest until the effects of the alcohol wear off naturally.

Some people believe that eating a big meal will keep a person sober, and drinking a glass of milk will coat the stomach and prevent alcohol from being absorbed. However, eating a meal or drinking a milk will not keep a person from getting drunk; food merely delays the rate at which alcohol will be absorbed into the bloodstream. If a person drinks too much alcohol, that person will get drunk, period. The only way to remain sober is to limit the consumption of alcohol.

Another fallacy is that all people have the same reactions to alcohol. People are not all the same, so they do not all react to the effects of alcohol in the same way. Many factors play a role in how an individual reacts to alcohol. Differences in body weight, gender, body chemistry, metabolism, and taking prescription medicines all affect the way a person's body reacts to alcohol.

One popular myth is that alcohol actually has food value and will give a person added energy. Alcohol is a depressant and slows the ability to think, move, and speak. It depresses or slows the functions of the mind and the body. Another excuse people make for drinking too much and abusing alcohol is that drugs are a bigger problem than alcohol. Because alcohol is a drug and has addictive properties, people can become addicted to alcohol as they would to any other drug.

Some adults as well as young people fall for the myth that it is no one's business if a friend drinks too much and that the drinker harms only himself or herself. A person who is an alco-

holic or a person who chooses to abuse alcohol affects the lives
of others. At the very least, family and friends are placed in the
uncomfortable position of having to deal with someone who
has a drinking problem. Also, the impaired judgment of an alcoholic can result in harm to others. If a person has an alcohol
problem, it is also a problem for friends and loved ones, so that
makes the drinking their business as well.

Types and Stages of Alcoholism

Addiction to alcohol does not come upon people all at once.
Sometimes it takes a while before people are aware that they
are drinking too much or too often, and it takes even longer for
some to admit they have a problem. The disease can build over
a period of time before the alcoholic or his friends or family are
aware of the problem. This is because just as there are many
different kinds of alcohol, alcoholism takes a variety of forms
and progresses through a number of stages.

Socially, alcoholic behavior can be divided into five groups.
Problem drinkers rely on alcohol to relieve stress. They drink
excessively, but not consistently. The problem drinker appears
to be able to control alcohol intake. Another type of alcoholic
is the hard drinker. Hard drinkers often have poor nutritional
habits. They tend to suffer from alcohol-related conditions,
such as gastritis and nerve degeneration. Hard drinkers appear
to be in control of their behavior, but many have poor job sta-
bility and place the safety and welfare of their families at risk.
Next are the periodic drinkers. Periodic drinkers can go long
periods of time without alcohol but then go on drinking binges.
They suffer from manic-depressive mood swings and lose control of their behavior when they drink. The main characteristic of plateau alcoholism, another behavior type, is the need
to maintain a constant level of alcohol in the body. This is the
prevalent type of alcoholism in parts of Europe and tends to
affect more women than men. Plateau alcoholics can hide their
conditions for years. Ultimately, though, plateau alcoholics
suffer serious health problems and lose their ability to control
their alcohol intake. Lastly, the majority of American alcoholics

fall into the category of steady alcoholism. Steady alcoholics suffer from psychological addiction, increased alcohol cravings, and, like periodic drinkers, lose control of their behavior when they drink.

These behavioral descriptions were derived in part from the research of Dr. E.M. Jellinek, one of the founders of the National Council on Alcoholism. He identified five basic types of alcoholism, which he named alpha, beta, gamma, delta, and epsilon. He named the least-damaging type of alcoholism for the first letter in the Greek alphabet, alpha, then continued with successive letters for progressively more serious forms of alcoholism. According to Jellinek, alpha alcoholics are psychologically dependent on alcohol. They rely on alcohol to relieve physical or emotional suffering. The alpha alcoholic might drink heavily enough to impair behavior but seldom totally loses control. Beta alcoholism can result in gastritis, liver problems, and nerve disorders, but beta alcoholics do not become physically or psychologically dependent on alcohol, and they do not have withdrawal symptoms when they stop drinking. Gamma alcoholics suffer the most serious physical and psychological damage. Gamma alcoholics can consume more alcohol without showing effects, but they progress from psychological to physical dependence and suffer frightening, sometimes physically uncomfortable withdrawal symptoms if they try to stop drinking. Sometimes, alpha and beta alcoholism can progress into gamma alcoholism.

As a rule, delta alcoholics do not lose control of their behavior, but they are unable to stay away from alcohol. They must maintain a constant level of alcohol in their bodies and cannot do without it for even brief periods of time. The fifth type of alcoholism described by Jellinek was epsilon alcoholism. The epsilon alcoholic may stay sober for weeks or months but sometimes goes on drinking binges for several days at a time.

Within any type of alcoholism, progression into worse problems can happen in stages. The pre-alcoholic begins with what appears to be innocent social drinking. This progresses until the person seeks out occasions to drink and consumes greater

amounts of alcohol during these opportunities. In the prodro-
mal phase, the person still has some control over drinking habits, but he or she is beginning to fall into a pattern. The early
stages of this phase can include reckless behavior and blackouts
(periods of time in which the person has no memory); drinking in secret; and hangovers consisting of headaches, nausea,
and sometimes vomiting. In the crucial phase, the alcoholic has
lost control over alcohol consumption. If the person takes even
one drink, the drinking will continue until the person is completely inebriated. This alcoholic makes excuses to drink and
has to rely on eye-openers, drinks of alcohol in the morning, to
begin the day. This phase can deteriorate into violent, destructive behavior. The chronic phase includes benders, which some
alcoholics call drinking to escape the problems caused by drinking. They may experience tremors and delirium tremens (DTs),
which are hallucinations with tremors. In this phase, the alcoholic's physical and mental states are seriously compromised,
and the person can become very ill or could die.

CHAPTER TWO

Dangers of Alcohol and Alcoholism

Some alcoholics become so desperate for a drink that they risk suffering serious side effects, even death, from consuming the wrong kind of alcohol. There are actually many different kinds of alcohol, but most would be dangerous or deadly if someone tried to drink them. For instance, isopropyl alcohol is used in cleaning products and skin lotion. Methyl alcohol is a component of paint remover and antifreeze. Consuming these kinds of alcohol can be fatal. The type of alcohol used in beverages, however, is called ethyl alcohol, or ethanol. Ethanol results when yeasts cause fermentation which converts the sugars in fruits, grains, and certain types of sugarcanes into alcohol. However, even though ethanol is drinkable, under certain conditions it can be toxic as well.

Full strength, ethanol has a harsh taste and causes a burning sensation in the mouth. For this reason ethanol is usually diluted in beverages. In addition to alcoholic beverages, ethanol is used in the preparation of varnishes and perfumes, to preserve biological specimens, as a fuel additive (gasohol), and as a disinfectant. It is also used in the preparation of some medicines.

Because of the physical properties of alcohol, alcoholics and others who misuse and abuse alcohol can experience physical problems ranging from mild side effects to serious health issues. This is because when consumed in excessive amounts, alcohol causes a variety of potentially dangerous reactions in the body. Side effects include dizziness, sleepiness, disorientation, and in extreme cases alcohol poisoning, a potentially fatal condition in which a toxic amount of alcohol has been consumed in a short period of time. The body's response to alcohol can be especially dangerous for people on medication, even over-the-counter medication. This is because alcohol can intensify the side effects of many medications. People who are currently taking prescription medication or even taking grocery store brand pain relievers or allergy medications should not consume beer, wine, or any other type of alcohol for the duration of the time they are taking the drugs.

The Body's Initial Reaction to Alcohol

One group, Teen Challenge of Southern California, describes the seriousness of alcohol's effects in this way: "If alcohol would have been invented today, you would need a prescription to obtain it or perhaps it would be outlawed completely."[10]

In addition to alcoholics, even people in good physical health who are on no medication whatsoever can suffer from the effects of excessive alcohol consumption. Alcohol travels directly from the stomach to the bloodstream. From there, it quickly travels to the brain, liver, and the rest of the body. Even though the liver helps rid the body of alcohol, sometimes people drink more than the liver can process. This is when alcohol builds up in the body and the person becomes impaired.

Intoxication does not affect all people at the same rate. For instance, in a man weighing about 160 pounds (72.57kg), the earliest symptoms of intoxication occur after about one drink. On the other hand, a 120-pound (54.43kg) woman may begin experiencing the same degree of side effects with only half a drink. So, with less than one drink, body systems begin to respond to the effects of alcohol. Even slight intoxication affects a person's ability to use machinery or drive safely.

When alcohol first hits the brain, the body's first response is usually a blissful state similar to euphoria, a feeling of happiness, enthusiasm, and sometimes talkativeness. This is caused by increased levels in the brain of a substance called dopamine. Some drinkers think that if one or two drinks make them feel happy and relaxed, several drinks will make them feel even better. After all, dopamine is the origin of the word "dope."

Alcohol also affects other chemicals in the brain. One is a chemical transmitter called serotonin. Serotonin affects memory, moods, and the ability to learn. Some researchers believe that increased levels of serotonin in the body contribute to a person's tendency to develop alcoholism. Additionally, alcohol controls the release of another brain chemical, gaba. Excessive amounts of gaba affect judgment, rational thinking, and body reflexes. When too much dopamine, serotonin, and gaba are released in the brain, the drinker is not able to control himself or herself. Besides the immediate effects, over time these chemicals can overproduce until the body's pleasure receptors no longer work naturally. Drinkers can no longer feel good without the presence of alcohol in their bodies. The abuse of alcohol can lead to some other very unpleasant short term effects as well, such as nausea and physical pain.

One of the most common ways the body responds to consuming excessive amounts of alcohol is an uncomfortable experience called a hangover. A hangover may include a headache, nausea, vomiting, fatigue, sore muscles, dizziness, and a dry mouth. Hangovers are caused by dehydration, especially to the brain. Dehydration causes temporary shrinkage in the brain, which pulls on pain-sensitive filaments that connect the brain to the skull. This is what causes the sensation of a blinding, skull-pounding headache. Alcohol acts as a diuretic on the body. Diuretics cause frequent urination, which removes sodium and potassium, elements the body needs in order to maintain optimal health and physical mobility. Both of these substances are important in the function of muscles and nerves. In addition to the painful headache, hangovers are also accompanied by uncomfortable stomach disturbances ranging from mild nausea to vomiting and diarrhea. This is the way the body rids itself of toxins and other substances that distress the digestive system. Some people suffer bouts of diarrhea and vomiting at the same time. Though hangovers are generally commonplace among heavy drinkers, they should not be taken lightly. They are actually serious disturbances to the body and body systems. In fact, hangovers are actually the physical symptoms of mild alcohol poisoning.

In some instances, people have allergic reactions to alcohol. Allergic reactions are the body's way of trying to protect itself from histamines. Histamines are substances found in plant and animal tissue that can trigger allergic responses in the human immune system, such as constriction of bronchial muscles, making it difficult for a person to breathe. These histamines occur in large amounts in red wines and to a lesser extent in white wines, beers, and some hard liquor.

Alcohol abuse also affects such issues as sleep patterns and weight gain. Alcoholics who pass out from drinking are not really sleeping. They do not get the quality rapid eye movement (REM) stage of sleep, which rests and refreshes the body. Because of this, the alcohol abuser wakes already tired and fatigued. In addition, many people do not consider all the calories they are taking in when they consume alcohol. Excessive alcohol consumption causes people to gain weight. A beer, for instance, contains 150 calories. These are empty calories because they have absolutely no nutritional benefit. For instance, if a person drinks up to four regular beers in one evening, that individual has consumed 600 useless calories. If such behavior becomes habit, drinking four beers a night several evenings a week can result in a 3- or 4-pound weight gain in one month's time. Basically, the digestive system takes on the calories, but the calories do not benefit the body. The calories simply add weight. The drinker may save a few calories by switching to light beer but not enough to prevent some weight gain. The weight gain may be slower, but weight gain cannot be avoided. An overweight alcoholic often has thin arms and legs but a large stomach. This is due to malnutrition, since the calories in alcohol have no food value. Many alcoholics suffer from malnutrition because they crave alcohol rather than food. Malnutrition is only one of the long-term effects of alcoholism.

Diseases and Organ Damage

Alcoholism can lead to diseases and other long-term health problems. Diseased body organs are examined by health researchers using special technology such as computed tomography (CT) and magnetic resonance imaging (MRI). These instruments can detect the earliest stages of organ damage.

Alcohol leads to weight gain that is often associated with the "beer belly."

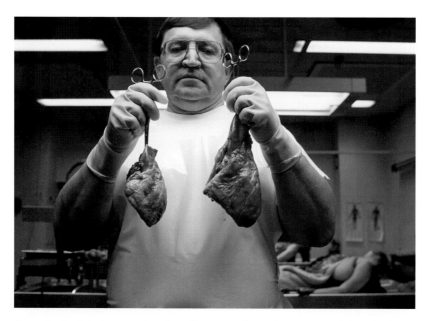

A pathologist shows a healthy liver on the right compared with the diseased liver of an alcoholic on the left.

If asked what organ-damaging disease is caused by alcoholism, most people think of cirrhosis of the liver. This is a condition in which normal healthy liver tissue is destroyed, leaving behind nonfunctioning scar tissue. Cirrhosis is just one liver disease linked to chronic use of alcohol. Fatty liver is another liver disease caused by alcoholism. Fatty liver is the excessive accumulation of fat in the liver cells that enlarges the liver and causes pain in the upper abdomen. Alcoholic hepatitis is another disease of the liver. This is acute inflammation of the liver in which individual cells are scarred and destroyed. A person suffering from alcoholic hepatitis may have a fever, an enlarged liver, yellowish-tinged skin (called jaundice), and an increase in white blood cells. Other symptoms of liver disease include spiderlike veins in the skin, an enlarged spleen, and kidney failure. Women alcoholics are at greater risk of liver disease than men and are over 50 percent more likely to die from the effects of liver disease than male alcoholics. This is because women tend to be smaller than men, so alcohol affects them faster and more strongly. Because of this, they are more susceptible to health problems from alcohol.

Some types of heart disease are also linked to alcoholism. However, a number of studies indicate that moderate alcohol consumption—for instance, one glass of red wine a day—helps prevent heart disease by raising HDL (good cholesterol) and lowering the accumulation of plaque in the arteries. Alcohol also helps keep blood platelets from clumping together and forming clots. Both of these can help reduce the risk of heart attack. There are better ways of strengthening and protecting the heart, such as healthy diet and exercise. If a drinker crosses the line between moderate and heavy alcohol consumption, this can actually lead to heart damage.

Long-term and excessive drinking can bring on high blood pressure, an enlarged heart, and other damage that can weaken the heart. Additionally, alcohol abuse can lead to strokes and congestive heart failure. One way excessive drinking harms the heart is by putting more fat into the circulatory system. This has the same effect on the heart as consuming large amounts of fried foods and other foods high in fat content.

Alcoholism and excessive drinking greatly reduce a person's chances for successful heart surgery or other treatments. Several alcohol-associated factors place the heart patient at higher risk. These include alcohol-related malnutrition, the depressant effects of alcohol, and general poor health that often accompanies alcohol addiction. Another reason an alcoholic can be a poor risk for surgery is because surgery is an invasive procedure, and one of the properties of alcohol is its ability to inhibit blood coagulation, which can cause the patient to hemorrhage. However, alcohol-related diseases are not limited to the heart and the liver.

Alcohol abuse affects the pancreas, as well. The pancreas is an organ near the liver and the stomach. The pancreas produces enzymes, which aid in the digestion of fat and protein and produces the hormones, insulin and glucagons, which keep blood sugar in balance. Alcoholism can lead to pancreatitis, a condition that causes the pancreas to swell and often

Mixing Alcohol with Medications

Many prescription medications carry warning labels about the dangers of drinking alcohol while taking certain prescribed medicines. These labels warn about the risks of driving an automobile or operating dangerous machinery. They also include the fact that alcohol might intensify the effect of the medication. However, these tiny warning labels barely touch the surface of the myriad of health dangers that can result from consuming alcohol while taking prescription or over-the-counter drugs.

Medications are usually a mixture of different chemicals. Any one of these chemicals can react negatively when they combine with alcohol in the body. Just as there are many different categories of medications to treat various illnesses and chronic conditions, combining these prescription drugs with alcohol can react on the body in a wide variety of ways. For instance, drinking alcohol while taking cold and flu medicines can intensify the dizziness and drowsiness associated with these drugs. Consuming alcohol while taking heart medications can cause a sudden change in blood pressure and fainting. Drinking while on arthritis medication can lead to stomach bleeding and liver problems, and combining alcohol with depression medication can actually intensify the depression to the point of suicide. The safest course to follow is to abstain from alcohol while taking any medications.

turn black or greenish. People with pancreatitis may suffer from high fever and debilitating stomach pain. In the worst of these conditions, they must be fed through intravenous tubes (IV). Since the person cannot take food by mouth, IVs send necessary nutrients directly into the blood. In fact, someone with pancreatitis may not be able to eat solid food for several months.

Most people do not realize that alcohol abuse is also linked to risks for developing certain kinds of cancers. Acetaldehyde is a substance formed in the body as alcohol is metabolized. Acetaldehyde is a suspected carcinogen, a cancer-causing agent. Some scientists conclude that some natural compounds that are essential for cell growth, called polyamines, react with the acetaldehyde to damage the body's DNA. This can result in the beginning stages of cancer. Polyamines usually protect the DNA, but when they react with acetaldehyde, a substance called crotonaldehyde is formed. In tests, this substance has been shown to cause cancer in animals and also causes DNA to mutate, or change. Excessive alcohol consumption triggers this chemical chain reaction in the body, increasing the risk of developing several different kinds of cancer.

The areas of the body that are at highest risk for developing alcohol-related cancer in both men and women are the mouth, pharynx, larynx, esophagus, liver, colon, and rectum. Additionally, a woman's risk of breast cancer is also increased by excessive alcohol consumption.

The brain is another organ at risk of permanent damage when a person abuses alcohol. One of the symptoms of a hangover is the severe headache caused by dehydration of brain tissue. In cases of prolonged alcohol abuse, the brain can be permanently damaged. This is caused by shrinkage in the area of the brain called the cortex of the frontal lobe. This is the part of the brain that controls higher intellectual function. Shrinkage also occurs in deeper areas of the brain, including those associated with memory, coordination, and balance. Another brain effect chronic drinkers may develop is a condition called Wernicke-Korsakoff's Psychosis. A person with this condition may experience confusion, hallucinations, paralysis, or all of these effects. In the worst instances, people with this condition can lose their memory. For instance, someone with Wernicke-Korsakoff's Psychosis could become hopelessly lost one block away from home. This particular symptom is something like Alzheimer's disease.

Alcohol abuse causes other health problems as well. It weakens the immune system, which makes alcoholics more susceptible to a variety of diseases including colds, flu, pneumonia, and even HIV and AIDS. This risk is especially dangerous since people under the influence of alcohol may not have good enough judgment to practice safe sex. This puts them at risk of contracting other sexually transmitted diseases. Also, since alcohol irritates the stomach lining, heavy drinkers can have heartburn, upset stomachs, and ulcers. Finally, excessive amounts of alcohol in the body impairs the absorption of calcium in the bones, which increases the risk of osteoporosis. People with osteoporosis have soft, brittle bones that break more easily than healthy bone tissue.

Alcoholism and Accidents

Alcoholics, or any people who consume too much alcohol, tend to have more accidents than non-alcoholics or non-drinkers.

Drunk drivers kill one American every 22 minutes.

More Americans have been killed in drunk-driving accidents than have died in all U.S.-involved wars since the Revolution.

This is because alcohol impairs coordination, balance, reflexes, and judgment. The more alcohol a person consumes, the more these skills are affected, and so the alcohol abuser has accidents. An accident may be something as simple as tripping on a door jamb and bumping an elbow or as catastrophic as a car crash. Alcohol abusers do not just harm themselves, they harm others as well.

Drunk drivers kill one American every 22 minutes. In addition to deaths, about 630,000 people are injured and nearly 30,000 of these accident victims will suffer permanent injuries. Statistics show that about three in every ten U.S. citizens will be in an alcohol-related car crash at some time in their lives. In fact, on any evening during the week, one out of fifty drivers is operating a vehicle while drunk. On weekend evenings, this number increases: one out of ten vehicles is operated by a drunk driver. To get an idea of how catastrophic a problem drunk driving is, consider this: the death rate is equal to one Boeing 747 aircraft carrying more than 500 passengers crashing every eight days, killing all passengers and crew. In fact, one half of all traffic accidents in the United States are alcohol-related. This means more Americans have been killed in drunk driving car crashes than have died in all of the U.S.-involved wars since the founding of this country.

Not only are drunk drivers' and their victims' lives changed, but sometimes so are the people who served the alcohol. For example, one young woman hosted a party in which alcohol was served. A young, male party guest drank too much and quickly became out of control. Although the host made arrangements for the guest to spend the night, the guest became belligerent, somehow got his friend's truck keys, and took the vehicle without permission. Almost immediately, he wrecked the truck and was badly injured. Since the woman had served the alcohol, she was held partially responsible for the accident. She later told a newspaper reporter the hard lesson she had learned as a result of the accident:

I don't think people realize the importance of having a

Alcohol and the Aging Body

Some research has shown that as people age, alcohol can have a more intense effect on their bodies, even on older people who are in good health. As people age, their reflexes begin to slow. Since alcohol affects the reflexes, drinking can place older people at great risk of accidental injury. Loss of coordination is but one of the natural symptoms of aging that makes it more difficult to recognize the development of alcoholism in older people. When older people appear forgetful, friends and family members may overlook it and make allowances for it as simply another sign that their loved one is getting on in years, when in fact the forgetfulness may actually be a symptom of alcohol abuse.

Some people who have never consumed alcohol begin drinking later in life. For instance, some people start drinking after the death of a spouse to cope with loneliness and to help them sleep. Some begin drinking due to boredom and inactivity after they retire. If these people are also taking medication for age-related conditions, such as high blood pressure, heart disease, and diabetes, they place their lives at serious risk. To help prevent these risks, friends and family members should visit with them and telephone them frequently and observe them for any changes in behavior or habits.

Alcohol can have a more intense effect on people as they age.

designated driver. I always hear them talk about being OK to drive, but no one realizes how few drinks it takes not to be OK. . . . If that kid would have died, I would be in jail. It would be my fault. I really woke up after that."[11]

Besides taking lives, drunk driving accidents cost Americans about $45 billion in property damage every year. Another $70.5 billion goes to hospitalization, outpatient therapy, and other quality of life issues.

Alcoholism and alcohol abuse are responsible for many other kinds of accidents, a large number of which occur in the home. By some estimates, 2.6 million home accidents occur every year, resulting in four thousand deaths. Alcohol use accounts for about four hundred of these deaths. Household accidents result from such things as improper use of tools, home drowning, falls, and fires. Many alcoholics and other heavy drinkers also smoke, so many home fires occur when the inebriated person either nods off and passes out on the sofa or in bed while smoking or is too impaired and disoriented to properly extinguish the cigarette. The cigarette falls onto the sofa cushions or the sheets, igniting a fire, and the person is badly burned or killed. Frequently, this happens while the person is drinking alone, and there is no one else around to either respond to a fire alarm or remove the cigarette and quickly extinguish the fire. Often, these fires go far beyond harming the person who has passed out from drinking too much. They spread, causing extensive property damage and injuring or killing others. This type of accident can be especially catastrophic when people pass out while smoking and drinking in apartment buildings or in hotel or motel rooms.

Since people are both physically and mentally impaired when they drink heavily, many alcohol abusers are injured or killed in falls. Alcohol-related falls often happen on stairways. Since an inebriated person's reflexes and judgment are impaired, he is less likely to be able to protect himself in a fall than a sober person in the same situation. This means the drinker hits the stairs or the floor more heavily than a sober person would.

Alcoholics who smoke risk causing fires when they pass out drunk while smoking.

Because of this, alcohol abusers suffer more broken bones and head injuries in falls than non-drinkers.

Home accidents can occur for a variety of reasons regardless of whether a person is sober or inebriated, but alcoholics often double their chances of being injured or killed in a home accident. For instance, an inebriated person is twice as likely to have an accident when climbing a ladder or a tree, using tools (especially power tools), trying to do any electrical work, or while in a swimming pool or a bathtub or shower. In fact, alcohol abuse is responsible for nearly a dozen deaths from drowning in homes every year. Many of these drownings are due to slipping and falling into the water rather than passing out.

Alcoholism and alcohol abuse are responsible for a significant number of accidents as well as other problems in the workplace. About 6 percent of the American workforce are alcoholics. On the whole, alcoholics have a 4 to 8 percent higher absentee rate than non-alcoholics. Additionally, alcoholics and other heavy drinkers are two-to-three times more likely to be involved in industrial accidents. In fact, according to some studies, of all on-the-job accidents, about 22 to 25 percent are alcohol-related. In all, problem drinking costs employers

Many accidents in the home and workplace are the result of alcohol abuse.

$15 billion a year in accidents, absenteeism, and other problems.

Alcohol Abuse and Victims of Violence

Alcohol abuse and violent crimes often go hand in hand. On any given day, about five million crimes are committed in this country. About two million of these crimes are committed by alcohol-impaired offenders. Some are crimes of violence in which people are injured or killed. According to the U.S. Department of Justice, four out of every ten crimes of violence involve people who have consumed large amounts of alcohol and are out of control. Among these violent crimes are assault, murder, rape, and sexual abuse.

Much of the information about alcohol related crimes comes from victims and witnesses who observed the offenders drinking, saw their behavior, and smelled the alcohol on them. According to some accounts, alcohol-impaired offenders account for 55 to 75 percent of the homicides, 40 percent of the rapes, and 50 percent of the sexual abuse cases. In round numbers, alcohol abuse accounts for about 183,000 rapes and sexual assaults, 197,000 robberies, 661,000 aggravated assaults, and 1.7 million simple assaults.

Some studies correlate the number of alcohol outlets, such as liquor stores, bars, and clubs, in a community with the number of violent crimes and property damage in the community. One study in California concluded that the greater the number of bars in a neighborhood, the higher the assault rate. Accordingly, reducing the availability and the temptation of alcohol to alcoholics and alcohol abusers and adding special taxes to make it less affordable results in fewer violent crimes and fewer automobile crashes and other alcohol-related accidents. When communities take these measures to make alcohol less readily available and more expensive, they help reduce crime and other alcohol-related social problems.

These efforts do not stop the problem of alcoholism, though. A committed alcoholic will go wherever necessary to obtain alcohol, regardless of personal consequences or effects on the family. Frequently, the families of alcoholics are the most seriously affected victims of this particular form of substance abuse.

CHAPTER THREE

Alcoholism and the Family

Alcoholism affects families of all races, cultures, faiths, and economic groups. It affects not only the individual but all members of the family, particularly the children. Nearly one in five adult Americans grew up in a home with an alcoholic parent. Parents are children's first authority figures and the first people children look up to and try to emulate. Children in families where one or both parents abuse alcohol or other drugs do not have the stable home life of children whose parents are not substance abusers. This is because the alcoholic's drinking patterns often run in cycles, characterized by hours or days of drunkenness interspersed with days, weeks, or even months of sobriety. Despite the outward appearances the alcoholic family displays to the world, these children literally do not know what behavior to expect from their parents from the time they wake in the morning until they go to bed at night.

According to some estimates, about 75 percent of the problem drinkers in this country are men, so in a majority of instances, the father is the alcoholic parent. However, alcoholism among females appears to be on the rise, so at some point, alcoholic families may be equally balanced between problem-drinking fathers and mothers. Households in which both parents are alcoholics, however, are in the minority, at about 20 percent.

Children who grow up in alcoholic households can develop a distorted view of authority and have problems in school, such as disruptive behavior, and can show symptoms of depression. Some children of alcoholics have poor language and reasoning skills and may not feel successful, even those who are performing well academically. Some of these children also have problems developing healthy relationships when they become adults. Some children of alcoholics do not suffer the negative effects that others do. These are usually children who have positive relationships with other strong adult role models, such as aunts, uncles, grandparents, neighbors, or teachers.

Positive adult role models are especially important to the children of alcoholics. The family is a unique social structure, very different from that of other groups such as those at work or in clubs. For instance, if job situations become intolerable, people have options. They can update their resumes and go in

Alcoholism affects all members in the family, especially the children.

Positive role models are particularly important to children of alcoholics.

search of other employment. Usually, though, people do not resign from their families, even if a family member is an alcoholic and causing many problems. Children have little, if any, choice. They are physically a part of the family group until they are grown and able to support themselves and move to homes of their own. Even then, they usually retain relationships with other family members.

Stages in the Alcoholic Family

Many families dealing with alcoholism go through characteristic stages or phases. Not all families move directly from one stage to the next and some families become mired at certain stages and do not progress to sobriety. Also, families do not all progress through the stages at the same rate. Some families remain in certain stages longer than others.

In the earliest phase, non-alcoholic family members react to the behavior of the drinking parent. They may modify their own

Accidental Alcohol Poisoning and Children

Small children run a significantly greater risk of alcohol poisoning than adults in homes where alcoholic beverages are served. This is because the enzyme systems, which protect the body from some harmful substances, are not yet fully developed in children. As little as 5 to 20 grams of alcohol can be enough to kill a child. From aggressive and excited behavior, the child rapidly deteriorates and suffers breathing problems, cold sweats, falling body temperatures, convulsions, and finally death.

If a child has consumed alcohol, vomiting must be quickly induced. This is because alcohol is rapidly absorbed by the body. Seek emergency medical attention immediately so physicians can begin an IV solution to flush the rest of the toxins from the child's body.

To avoid the dangers of alcohol poisoning, all alcoholic substances should be stored and secured well out of the reach of children and alcoholic drinks should never be left unattended.

behavior to accommodate the drinker or avoid unpleasant or stressful confrontations. The alcoholic's drinking manipulates the family. At this stage, the entire family is in denial, just as the alcoholic is in denial. They develop coping strategies. The coping strategies family members develop at this stage may be more harmful than helpful to the alcoholic or the rest of the family. Some family members may fall into the emotional trap of believing that they are doing something that causes the alcoholic to drink. They may also blame themselves for the person's drinking. At this point, some family members may retreat from normal social interactions, such as spending time with friends or participating in church, clubs, or sports activities. They may also retreat emotionally in an effort to hide or protect their feelings or avoid relationships entirely.

In families with young children, the non-alcoholic parent may try to overcompensate or somehow make it up to the children because the other parent is emotionally unavailable and failing them. The sober parent may do this by totally ignoring the problem and treating the excessive drinking and the irrational and sometimes violent behavior that goes with it as typical family problems. This is similar to the analogy of ignoring the 600-pound gorilla in the living room. If they ignore it long enough, it may go away on its own. However, alcoholism, as well as the wide range of social, economic, and health-related problems that accompany it, seldom goes away on its own. By denying the problem exists, the family delays getting the help it needs.

A major step in moving beyond this destructive stage is when the family is ready to admit that denying alcoholism does not make the problem go away. The family members are able to recognize the negative effects the parent's alcoholism has on each individual in the family. They come to understand that they are not responsible for causing the person to drink, and they do not have to continue to modify and compromise their behavior to fit that of the alcoholic. They realize they need help as a family and become active in their own recovery process, realizing that help is available and they do not have to be alone.

During this stage, the non-alcoholic family members may choose to resume normal family activities, whether the alcoholic is trying to quit drinking at this point, or not. If the alcoholic continues drinking, it may slow the family's progression through this stage, but if the sober family members are determined to move on with their lives, the alcoholic's behavior will not prevent it. For instance, the sober parent may encourage the children to return to school and sporting activities and seek out self-help groups for the family. By doing this, they may give up some of their anonymity by trying to hide or protect the alcoholic. The fact that a parent is an alcoholic may become public knowledge, but by taking this step, the rest of the family has begun an emotional separation from the alcoholism. They may still live with an alcoholic, but at the very least they have given themselves permission to feel normal once again.

If the alcoholic parent has not made the decision to seek help and make changes by this time, the family may face a very difficult decision: whether or not to physically remove themselves from the alcoholic environment. In this stage, family members may choose sides. The non-alcoholic may threaten the alcoholic parent with divorce and taking away the children. This hectic and turbulent period causes some children a great deal of stress. Sometimes their loyalties are torn and they become angry and resentful toward both parents. For other children, however, they may feel that the alcoholic parent was already essentially missing from their lives, and being rid of all the problems that go along with living with an alcoholic might come as a relief. In this case, change is a benefit rather than a trauma.

By this time, the family unit has begun to reorganize as a single-parent household. If the alcoholic parent is still drinking, though, he or she may try to manipulate the family dynamics by using the children against the non-alcoholic parent, especially the younger children who may have been sheltered from the worst of the family turmoil and still want the parents to be together. During this family reorganization, especially if a manipulative drinking parent is still part of the picture, the family needs special support to keep from falling back into unhealthy patterns.

One recovering alcoholic father described the importance of alcohol compared to his relationship with his wife and children, saying, "I had to have that drink. Nothing else mattered, not my wife, my kids, nothing. It was alcohol above everything."[12]

Some alcoholic families stall in one of these stages and never achieve unity because they are not able to emotionally distance themselves from the drinking parent's destructive behavior. The family may be able to successfully reunite as a whole, including the alcoholic parent, if that parent chooses to get help and stop drinking. There are pitfalls here too, however. For years, the family may have been blaming all of its problems on alcoholism. Some may believe that all problems disappear when alcohol goes away and that life will somehow be perfect. This is not reality. The family has not had the opportunity to experience the average problems of a normal family, and when they occur, family members may need help learning to deal with them. There is also the possibility that the alcoholic may backslide into abusive drinking habits. This makes it difficult for some family members to trust the efforts the parent is making or to believe the alcoholic parent can change.

True healing does not happen until the family comes to terms with the recovering alcoholic. This means putting the wrongs, betrayal, and all aspects of the alcoholic parent's former behavior in the past, which is a very difficult thing to do when trust has been violated time after time. Each member of the family must first come to terms with how alcoholism has affected him or her personally. Often, this requires the help of a therapist, group counseling, or some sort of support group. If the recovering alcoholic can maintain sobriety, if the family can forgive, and if they can adjust to changes, sometimes in roles within the family, they have a good chance of continuing to grow and strengthen as a family unit.

Adapting and Changing Roles

One parent assuming sole responsibility for the welfare of the entire family is often overwhelming. Sometimes the parent comes to rely on one or more of the children to act as the family's second-in-command. This is often the role of the oldest daughter, or if there are no daughters, the oldest son. The second-in-command role is a time-consuming one. The son or daughter in this role usually does not participate in sports or other extracurricular activities. After-school hours are filled with looking after younger siblings and taking care of the house while the non-alcoholic parent, usually the mother, earns income to support the family. Even if the non-alcoholic parent is the father, the second-in-command child must fill the same role, because the alcoholic mother is often not in a physical or mental state to care for the younger children, cook, or clean house. Even after all of the younger children are grown and leave the house, this parent's helper may be slow to form personal adult relationships and will likely marry late if at all. This is because the child has spent a lifetime putting the welfare and needs of others first and has seldom thought in terms of his or her own personal choices and happiness.

Children of alcoholics may assume a variety of other roles as well. Some do everything they can to make the family appear normal to the outside world. These children work hard to be high achievers while in school and later, as adults, are very successful in their chosen careers. This success can be hollow, though, if the adult child of an alcoholic feels like an undeserving impostor who is not entitled to personal happiness or professional success because of family history. Other children cope with the chaos of an alcoholic home life by emotionally disappearing. These children do not want to be noticed, because attracting the attention of the alcoholic parent can sometimes be a very bad thing. These children are often shy, quiet, and avoid any kind of recognition as they try to become invisible.

Another coping strategy children of alcoholics might attempt is taking on the role of the family peacemaker, trying to smooth over all of the family's problems. Like the second-in-command, the peacemaker puts the needs of others over personal feelings. Another child in the same family, frequently a son, might respond to alcoholic home life in a totally different manner, by attracting attention in negative ways. For example, he might steal, skip school, get into fights, vandalize property, or possibly use alcohol and other drugs. As his behavioral problems escalate, this is often an indicator that problems are also escalating at home. If this child remains in the same behavior patterns until he is grown, he may also become an alcoholic or be addicted to other drugs. He will likely work in a series of low-paying jobs or could have trouble holding down a job, and he may become an abusive spouse or parent.

Whatever role children in alcoholic families assume, they tend to develop certain traits, such as mistrustfulness. After all, a parent, someone they should be able to trust and depend on has let them down for years, so why should they trust an adult or anyone else? Experience has taught them it is safer not to feel anything, because the emotions they have seen expressed at home are often out of control and destructive. They have also learned it is safer not to talk about their feelings, because someone could get upset with them. Many of these children have little or no self-esteem, because they have lacked adult role models to teach them how to respect themselves. Without the proper help, these dysfunctional children may become maladjusted adults, continuing the cycle of alcoholism, abuse, and violence. In fact, children of alcoholics are four times as likely to become alcoholics themselves than children of non-alcoholics.

Physical abuse is often a fact of life in an alcoholic household.

Family Violence and Other Side Effects of Alcoholism

Living with alcoholism can go far beyond taking up the slack with household responsibilities when the alcoholic parent is out of control. Some alcoholics become violent. They may take out their hostilities on furniture, doors, walls, or on people. Family abuse is often a fact of life in an alcoholic household. In fact, according to a study conducted in the 1990s, over 50 percent of male alcoholics have been violent toward their female partners at some time or other. Also, Intimate Partner Violence, or IPV, seems to occur most often in marriages in which the couple argued frequently in the earliest months of their marriage, and the male partner later developed heavy drinking habits, while the woman did not. Frequently, arguing over the amount the husband drinks and how much money he spends on alcohol leads up to the violence. Not all IPV is male-to-female, though. Female-to-male assaults account for 15 percent of the assaults among white couples, 21 percent of assaults among Hispanic couples, and 30 percent of assaults among African American couples. However, the violence in alcoholic families is not limited to the parents.

While child abuse can and does happen in families with non-alcoholic parents, it is six times more likely to occur in alcoholic families. Sometimes the alcoholic parent attacks the children. Sometimes the children are too small to defend themselves.

A teenage child describing abuse by a violent alcoholic parent, said,

> He had me down, pounding me in my face. I can't tell you how many times he beat the crap out of me when I was little, just a little kid. I decided this time, well, he just wasn't going to do it to me any more. I got away from him and got the gun. I didn't really want to hurt him. I just didn't want him hurting me any more. I had the thing pointed right at his face. It was like he couldn't believe I'd actually stand up to him. That's the only time I remember seeing him scared of anything. And it was me he was scared of.

The alcoholic abuser is often, but not always, the man.

If my grandma hadn't talked me down, I think maybe I really would have killed him. I guess he got the message, because he never took his fists to me again.[13]

Lifetime Side Effects of the Alcoholic Family

Leaving home is not a sure escape from alcoholism. Even when children of alcoholics become adults and move out of the family home, many do not escape the effects of having grown up in an alcoholic household. The damage has already been done. Many adult children of alcoholics have problems with depression and violence and show a higher incidence of developing mental disorders later in life. Some become addicted to substances themselves. They may experience difficulties in developing healthy, stable adult relationships and have trouble handling responsibilities. Some make unsuccessful parents.

This is not to say that adult children of alcoholics are doomed to be failures. Some are able to emotionally distance themselves from the cycle of alcoholism without any sort of counseling and live rewarding, productive lives. Others may not be able to cope on their own and require professional counseling. With the right kind of help, adult children of alcoholics can break the destructive cycle of alcoholism.

Sometimes the violent alcoholic will assault elderly family members who, like children, cannot fight back. The elderly are often afraid to speak up, because they have nowhere else to go. They would rather take the abuse than face the unknown. Some elderly family victims of alcoholic assault do not report the assaults because they feel that the alcoholism is a shameful family secret that must be hidden at all costs.

Another destructive side effect some alcoholic families suffer is incest, which include sexual assaults against younger family members. Usually, these assaults are father-against-daughter. Thirty percent of all sexual assaults against female children are alcohol-related. Incest has horrendous long-term effects. Many child victims of incest grow up to become anxiety-ridden, mistrustful, and fearful of authority figures. They engage in sexually promiscuous behavior and often become substance abusers themselves.

While some alcoholic families are dealing with violence and other types of physical and emotional damage, many have serious economic problems as well. In fact, alcoholism frequently places a heavy financial burden on families, especially families where the father is the alcoholic. In most traditional family structures, the father is the primary provider. In families where the father is the alcoholic, one of the consequences could be a major or a total loss of family income. In the earliest stages of alcoholism, the father may be able to mask the effects of his drinking from his co-workers and his superiors. After months or sometimes years of alcohol abuse, though, alcoholism ultimately affects the father's job. He may be passed over for promotions, demoted, or put on temporary suspension. He also could be fired from his job. If the mother has a job that pays a good salary, the family may be able to survive financially by just dropping extras, like family vacations, movies, club memberships, and athletic associations. If, however, the mother has a low-paying job or does not work outside the home, the family could be in serious trouble. They may have to move from their home to an apartment or move in with relatives. In worst cases, some families have had to move into shelters.

Alcohol and Unborn Children

While alcoholic fathers bring many hardships to their families, alcoholic mothers create their own unique problems, particularly alcoholic women who are pregnant. Expectant mothers who drink or abuse drugs place their unborn children at serious risk of a variety of serious health problems. Babies of alcoholic mothers can be born prematurely or significantly underweight. They can also be born with conditions that will affect their entire lives.

One of these conditions is Fetal Alcohol Syndrome, or FAS. The presence of alcohol in the mother's body slows the growth

Pregnant women who drink can cause their babies to have serious defects or health problems.

and development of the fetus. FAS children frequently have lower than average intelligence and are slow in developing their motor skills. These problems result from the usually poor health of the alcoholic mother as well as the fact that the alcohol travels through the mother's bloodstream into the umbilical cord and into the body of the unborn child.

Children who were born to alcoholic mothers are also more likely to have other problems, ranging from Attention Deficit Disorder, or ADD, to brain damage, which is sometimes so severe that the child does not survive long after birth. Children with ADD are easily distracted. They have difficulty concentrating, and sometimes get into trouble in school for not paying attention. Children with severe brain damage may never be able to walk, talk, or even sit up. Frequently, they do not live to be very old and many of these children are so severely handicapped they must spend their lives in medical institutions.

Even if the child of the alcoholic mother is born normal, there are often later complications. Adult daughters of alcoholic mothers can have problems with their own pregnancies. They often give birth prematurely to underweight babies. Even if the babies survive birth, the incidence of infant mortality among these premature babies is higher than average.

These dismal futures do not await all children of alcoholics, but children of alcoholic families do have significantly higher chances of being victims of violence or other abuse and have a greater chance of being born with handicaps. Without proper intervention and supervision, these children may become alcoholics themselves before they are even legally old enough to purchase alcohol.

CHAPTER FOUR

Alcoholism and Peer Pressure

In 2002, the Center on Addiction and Substance Abuse announced that underage drinkers were responsible for 25 percent of the alcohol consumed in the United States. Some argue, however, that since this figure includes 18 to 20-year-olds (young people who are old enough to live independently, vote, marry, and serve in the armed forces), to imply that children are drinking this much alcohol is misleading. The fact is, though, that the legal age to purchase alcoholic beverages in nearly every state is 21. This is the law. People under 21 who are able to slide by the system and buy alcohol with fake IDs are breaking the law.

It is also a fact that alcohol dependence among young people is a serious issue. According to the National Institute on Alcohol Abuse and Alcoholism, young people who begin drinking alcohol before age 16 are four times as likely to become alcohol-dependent than people who wait until the age of 21 to begin consuming alcohol. Some children begin drinking in their later years of elementary school or early in junior high. Among young people who drink, a significant number of children in their early teens are already in early stages of alcohol dependency.

Some young people start drinking alcohol because they have the mistaken idea that drinking makes them more mature. For others, drinking alcohol is one symptom of rebellious behavior, like fighting with parents, breaking curfew, driving too fast and recklessly, or hanging out with friends their parents don't like. While drinking and rebelliousness may be only a phase, it can also lead to much more serious problems. Alcohol abuse contributes to chronic depression, personality disorders, and even the death rate among teens and young adults. In fact, alcohol is the leading cause of fatal automobile accidents, suicides, and homicides in young people ages 15 to 24.

Alcohol abuse among young people is a serious issue.

Enhancing the Appeal of Alcohol

In the mid 1990s, some alcohol manufacturers began producing a new line of alcoholic beverages called designer drinks. According to some research, these drinks are particularly attractive to people under the age of eighteen. One appeal of these designer drinks is their cheap price, which sometimes cost little more than common soft drinks. Another attraction is the range of flavors, which masks the true taste of alcohol. Most young people do not like the taste of alcohol on its own. The sweetening and flavoring hides the taste, making it more palatable. This increases the likelihood that young people will drink until they are intoxicated. These designer drinks have come under public scrutiny, raised concerns about the health and safety of young people, and led some groups to demand that the advertising of such drinks be curtailed if not banned.

Some alcohol manufacturers sell sweet, flavored designer drinks, which appeal to young people.

Alcohol Abuse Among Children and Teens

According to statistics about people who consume alcohol, boys take their first drinks of alcohol at about 11 years old. Girls tend to take their first drinks later, when they are about 13. About three-fourths of the young people in the United States will try alcohol sometime between the ages of 11 and 18. Most will not develop drinking problems. Many will not touch alcohol again after their first taste. Their home environment largely determines how they behave toward alcohol after that first step. Children's attitudes toward drinking alcohol are closely linked to the behavior of their parents regarding alcohol. Even in households where adults drink in moderation, children who have close relationships with their parents and whose parents have warned them about the dangers of alcohol and drug abuse are less likely to become alcohol-dependent.

On the other hand, the opposite tends to be true in households with children who do not have good relationships with their parents or children who lack parental supervision, support, and communication. This seems to be the case even among children in families who do not drink. Households where parents show little concern and are neglectful are usually linked to heavy drinking and drunkenness among young people. Alcohol problems also occur among children whose parents give them the impression that they are not good enough, smart enough, or successful enough. Children and teens tend to seek out people and environments where they feel accepted. If they feel accepted among groups who abuse alcohol and other drugs, they will likely participate in that behavior, too. Children who already feel they do not meet expectations and also live in households with alcoholic parents have a far greater chance of falling into alcohol abuse themselves than children from non-drinking families.

Whether their parents drink or not, all children face conflicts and challenges as they grow up. Average and even especially bright children sometimes have problems in school, but children with learning disabilities face even more difficulties. They already feel inferior, and if they are taunted by classmates or feel that they are letting down or disappointing their parents, they feel even worse. Regardless of where they receive negative signals, these children are hurting, and, like some adults, they may turn to alcohol to stop the pain. They may sneak alcohol from their parents or get it from their friends' homes. Children with learning disabilities have a number of issues in

Factors Influencing Drinking in College

Some students will begin drinking or even become alcohol abusers when they move away from home and family influence and enter college life. Others will not. The likelihood of developing risky behaviors, such as alcohol abuse, depends on a number of physical, psychological, cultural, and social factors. For instance, a student from an alcoholic household is more likely to participate in drinking activities than a student whose family does not drink. Some families do not drink because it is against their religion or because people of their particular culture do not drink. Other families choose not to drink because they believe that alcohol is unhealthy. On the other hand, some students drink because, like some adults, there is something in their bodies that craves alcohol. For others, drinking may be a symptom of a compulsive behavior disorder. Still others drink because they think it will help them fit in with certain groups. Many college campuses are working to provide early intervention for student drinking problems.

common with children of alcoholic families. They may feel lonely, depressed, and have low self-esteem. These three factors are closely related to alcohol abuse.

Other paths to alcohol abuse can also be traced back to parental behavior. Children mimic the behavior of their role models, and the first role models children usually see are their parents. If children see their parents abusing alcohol, behaving irrationally, and driving drunk, they come to believe this is normal behavior, because this is the only adult behavior these small children have had the opportunity to observe.

As children get a little older, they try to mimic the behavior of other people they admire. At one time, famous people hid their misbehavior. This is not the case now, thanks to the media. For instance, children can see their favorite singers, actors, beauty queens, and athletes drinking, carousing, and fighting on television and read about it in newspapers and fan magazines. If these episodes are all over the news, in the judgment of some young fans, this is acceptable behavior. If famous, popular people are getting drunk and getting into fights, it must be okay. After all, if the cool people are doing it, it must be the cool thing to do. What children do not see, however, is the weeks or months in rehabilitation facilities and the toll alcohol abuse ultimately takes on these stars' health and their careers. By the time one young pop star disappears into a treatment facility, another one has come along to take his or her place in the limelight.

Regardless of what leads them to drink, underage alcohol abusers do not drink like adult alcoholics. Adult alcoholics will drink alone. Some drink on a daily basis. Most young problem drinkers confine their heavy drinking to the weekends and drink among friends. Although some young alcoholics do drink alone, they are in the minority.

Young people abuse alcohol differently, and their bodies respond to alcohol differently than those of adults. Since children are smaller than adults, alcohol's effects occur faster. The smaller the body mass, the faster the person becomes dizzy and disoriented. In addition to feeling the effects of alcohol sooner, children can suffer serious and permanent damage to their bodies. Scientists believe that the human brain continues to develop until about age 16. Research shows that underage drinking slows brain development in people under 21. Young problem drinkers also have trouble concentrating in school, especially in developing math skills. Some develop permanent problems with motor skills as well.

In the lives of children and teens, peer pressure can be a constant stumbling block. In order to avoid the social and health problems of alcohol abuse, children and young adults need the help of responsible adults both at home and at school in building their social skills. Children with well-developed social skills are more likely to feel confident in saying no to drinking alcohol as well as any other risky behavior. They need to be taught that drinking and driving is never acceptable, and they should never get in the car with a driver who has been drinking. They need to learn that drinking games are irresponsible and dangerous and that getting drunk puts their health and safety at risk. Children and teens also need to learn how to be able to refuse alcoholic drinks firmly but politely. They need to understand that the kind of people who serve alcohol to underage people or encourage underage drinking do not think about the dangerous consequences. These may not be the best people to choose as friends.

Alcohol Abuse in College

Problems with underage drinking do not end when students graduate from high school. If students go directly from high school to college, most people are 22 years old by the time they complete four years of college and earn their bachelor's degrees. That means they have been legally able to buy and consume alcohol for only the last year of their college careers. Nevertheless, out of control drinking is a major problem on many college campuses today.

Joseph Califano, head of the National Center on Addiction and Substance Abuse at Columbia University in New York, notes that "Basically the proportion of college students who drink and binge drink has stayed constant. But what's troubling is the tremendous increase in the intensity of their drinking and drug use and the excessiveness of it."[14]

Many of these problems come from activities college students treat as traditions, or rites of passage toward adulthood. In fact, some people see excessive drinking and drinking games as a part of the college culture. Sometimes, though, these drinking games end in death, and the students never get to become adults. One article published in 2004 in a major national magazine described the deaths of five college students in four states. It appeared the students drank themselves to death in separate binge drinking episodes. One of the students, a 19-year-old

In college, alcohol abuse is a common problem and often leads to tragic results.

girl, was said to have consumed nearly forty beers and shots of vodka on the evening she died.

Altogether, about seventeen hundred college students die each year from binge drinking and other alcohol-related incidents, such as falls and automobile accidents. An additional 600,000 are injured in accidents while under the influence of alcohol, and nearly 700,000 are assaulted by alcohol-impaired students.

By definition, male students are binge drinking when they consume five or more drinks in a row. For women it is four or more drinks. As most students admit, binge drinking is basically an excuse for getting drunk. Over half of the students who participate in binge drinking do so three or more times in a two-week period. Binge drinking can be fatal, but there are other consequences to this destructive behavior. Students frequently miss classes and fall behind in school work. Some of them damage property, hurt others, or get injured. They also get into trouble with the campus police and often drive drunk.

The binge drinker is not the only one who suffers as a result of his irresponsible behavior, though. Friends and roommates also experience the fallout. They frequently lose sleep and have to take care of the intoxicated student. Some are physically assaulted or have their property damaged. Binge drinking also contributes to rape and other forms of sexual assault.

If students become heavily involved in binge drinking, this behavior can quickly develop into alcoholism. According to research results released in 2005 from a three-year study by The National Survey on Drug Use and Health, nearly 17 percent of all college students are heavy drinkers. Of this percentage, nearly twice as many male students as female students abuse alcohol. Despite the information about alcoholism and the substance abuse programs available on campuses around the country, young people in college who are alcohol abusers are less likely to seek treatment than alcoholic adults in the workforce.

In an interview for the Lowe Family Foundation Web site, which is dedicated to helping families cope with alcoholism, Gina Poggione, Director of the Office of Alcohol and Drug Education at Notre Dame, spoke of factors relating to the dangers of high-risk alcohol consumption among college and university students:

> Students who are high-risk drinkers are drinking on empty stomachs, mixing with medication, drinking large quantities in a short amount of time, drinking with a gigantic family history, or in an abusive manner. All of that would be considered high risk drinking."[15]

One problem is in getting students to take alcohol abuse seriously by making them realize that alcohol abuse is a danger rather than a sign of becoming an adult or a celebration of freedom from parental control. Some students are under the mistaken impression that everyone on the campus drinks alcohol, and if they want to fit in to college life they should drink, too. This leads some young people to go against their own family values and traditions. On some campuses, within the first few weeks of school, nearly two-thirds of freshmen students who come from non-drinking families begin drinking with their classmates.

Alcohol abuse on campus leads to problems beyond going against personal family values. Since excessive alcohol consumption interferes with judgment and lowers inhibitions, some students become involved in behavior they probably would not participate in if they were sober. For instance, the average person would not consider running down a public street wearing no clothes, but this activity, once called streaking, is still a tradition on some campuses. On two fairly well-known northern college campuses, some students, most of whom have had too many drinks, shed their clothing and frolic outdoors in the middle of winter as part of unofficial college traditions. In addition to arrests for public lewdness and public intoxication, some of these students have to be hospitalized for hypothermia and frostbite.

Alcohol abuse at school events can sometimes lead to consequences more serious than public drunkenness and a brief hospital stay. Drinking played a major role in reducing a long-standing tradition on one southern college campus to a scene of carnage. There, drinking during the building of the traditional bonfire structure contributed to an accident in which twelve students were crushed to death and another twenty-seven were injured. For many years, students arranged hundreds of logs into a massive bonfire structure intended to burn just before their season's final football game, one with their archrival. In 1999, the bonfire framework, made of 500-pound (226.8kg) tree trunks, towered to a height of 60 feet (18.29m) before the two-ton structure collapsed. Although alcohol was supposed to be prohibited during the construction, a number of beer cans were photographed strewn around the site after the collapse. Two of the victims who had been working on the structure were found to have high levels of alcohol in their blood.

One of the Texas Alcoholic Beverage Commission investigators who examined the site of the tragedy remarked,

> You've got people drinking beer while putting together a complex structure. You have to wonder if, over the years, that isn't what caused the change in structure, the hand-me-downs of instructions from students getting convoluted while under the influence.[16]

Poor judgment and lowered inhibitions brought on by alcohol abuse also leads to irresponsible sexual activity. Some alcohol abusers drink to the point they do not remember if they even consented to having sex. According to some records, 400,000 college students engage in unprotected sex each year due to alcohol abuse. At the very least, college students who abuse alcohol can make errors in judgment for which they later become ashamed. They can fail classes, inconvenience their friends, or injure themselves. They may even spend time in jail for choosing to abuse alcohol. Arrests records can cast shadows on future careers.

Legal Consequences of Underage Drinking

People do not make their best decisions when they are under the influence of alcohol. This seems to be especially true of young people. One parent, an attorney, tells about a trespassing charge issued against his teenage daughter one evening when she had been drinking: "One night I got a call from the police station because my daughter was caught entering an open window at a local university. She was drunk with some friends and they were trying to bypass paying for a concert that was going on in a gym."[17]

This parent made a hard decision. He chose to allow his daughter to face the consequences of her actions. He did not try to have the charges dropped. It was a humiliating experience for her, but it was a serious wakeup call. Drunk or sober, people are responsible for their behavior.

Alcohol abuse can result in serious legal consequences for both adults and minors, but the very act of purchasing or publicly consuming alcohol is against the law for anyone under the age of 21 in nearly every state in the United States. For instance, in Texas, if a minor attempts to purchase alcohol, drink alcohol, or is caught in possession of alcohol, the first offense is a fine of up to $500, a mandatory alcohol awareness course, 8 to 12 hours of community service, and a thirty-day license suspension. Possession of a fake identification, usually used to purchase alcohol, carries a fine of up to $200. Trying to change information on a legal driver's license is called tampering with governmental record. This is a felony offense that can send a person to prison for two to ten years and/or levy a fine of $10,000. The legal consequences are the same for manufacturing counterfeit identification.

The State of Illinois will suspend a minor's driver's license for up to a year if that person is caught purchasing, drinking, or in possession of alcohol. Many other states carry the same penalties. In Maryland, underage drinking fines begin at $500 for a first offense, climbing to $1,000 for repeat offenses. Of course there are exceptions to laws governing underage drinking. If the minor is involved in a religious activity, like communion, in which wine is served in some faiths, and is accompanied by a parent or legal guardian who is also participating, the consumption of alcohol is legal. Otherwise, any minors caught purchasing, drinking, or possessing alcohol in a public place can expect to be taken to a juvenile detention facility or jail and kept there until a parent, a guardian, or an attorney can be contacted to come to the facility and discuss the minor's legal consequences.

Alternatives

To avoid such consequences, minors should stay away from alcohol. In fact, many groups are forming alliances to help young people stay sober. Colleges, health agencies, religious organizations, and communities are working together to provide healthful alternatives to events that involve consuming excessive amounts alcohol and other potentially dangerous behavior. Some of these efforts include public service advertising campaigns, which spell out the legal and safety consequences of abusing alcohol. They get the point across that getting drunk is not cool. Many colleges now contact parents when students, even those who have not had run-ins with the police, appear to have drinking problems, and many campuses have alcohol-free dormitories for undergraduates. Some colleges are leading the way in changing attitudes about alcohol abuse.

For instance, the Massachusetts Institute of Technology (MIT) has been a leader in improving campus alcohol policies and working with the surrounding Boston/Cambridge community to detect students with alcohol or other drug problems and refer them for help. MIT has worked with the community to produce a brochure of alcohol-alternative activities in the area and distributed it to all first year students. In the past, these activities have included the January 2000 Millennium Ball, which drew over two thousand participants, and the "Battle of the Bands" night at the House of Blues, a Cambridge area restaurant in 2002. Additionally, all first-year students are required to live on campus, and several on-campus fraternities have volunteered to be alcohol-free.

Since MIT has many students who are over 21, there are also events at which alcohol is served. A number of strict policies govern these events, including registering alcohol-related events with the appropriate authorities; not allowing student organization funds to be used to purchase alcohol; designating personnel for security purposes and to monitor drinking and behavior at the event; and insuring that servers are 21 or older. Additionally, organizers must sign a special alcohol guidelines form, which spells out the campus rules governing alcohol-associated events.

At the University of Wisconsin at Madison, bar owners near the university have agreed not to have ladies' nights or cheap, two-for-one drink specials, which draw students. To violate this agreement, the bars risk losing their licenses. In 2001, the university took a stand against alcohol abuse at sporting events. It pledged not to allow beer to be sold at its new athletic stadium, a financial loss estimated at $500,000 during hockey season alone. Many other such policies are now in effect or in the process of being implemented in college and university communities throughout the country.

CHAPTER FIVE

Roads to Recovery and the Power of Knowledge

Many alcoholics and other substance abusers reach a time in their lives called hitting bottom. Hitting bottom means the person has reached a very low point physically and emotionally. This is the point at which the alcoholic is finally ready to admit his or her addiction and is ready to seek help. For some, being arrested for driving under the influence (DUI) is the wakeup call. For others, it takes something much more serious to awaken the alcoholic to the fact that he or she needs help. This could mean the person may have become homeless; may have lost the support, respect, and trust of family and friends; or may have health issues that are serious enough to be life threatening. The person may have even attempted suicide. When a person is at this stage, however, the only direction to go is up. The journey can be very difficult, and the road to recovery can have many ruts and bumps. One person described her personal journey toward recovery during her earliest months and years of sobriety, and the backsliding thoughts she referred to as "stinking thinking":

In early sobriety and for a couple of years after I quit drinking . . . those billboards with the icy cold beer made me froth at the mouth, especially on a hot summer day . . . those advertisements on TV kicked in my stinking thinking (boy, wouldn't that be nice . . .) and I had to turn the channel, and it seemed like every movie I watched people were pouring down the alcohol . . . couldn't watch them either. . . . I avoided going down the aisle in the grocery store where "the alcohol" was shelved. Listening to those "cryin' in your beer, country music songs" got me started, too. Early on, just the smell of alcohol was enough to start my stinking thinking, so the actual image of it wreaked more havoc within my sick brain . . . "[18]

Despite the long and difficult nature of the recovery process, though, when the alcoholic makes the decision to change, there are many kinds of self-help groups, counseling agencies,

Alcoholics Anonymous (AA) is known worldwide for its self-help support groups.

Drugs for the Treatment of Alcoholism

Alcohol and drugs do not mix. However, drugs have been developed for use in the treatment of alcoholism. One of these drugs, Vivitrol, was approved by the Federal Food and Drug Administration in April 2006. Given in injection form, Vivitrol appears to turn off the craving for alcohol. A version of this drug in oral form has been in use for more than ten years. Physicians believe that this drug works by blocking the brain's neurotransmitters that are linked to alcohol dependence. While Vivitrol is not a sure cure, physicians report a promising percentage of success with this drug among patients being treated for alcoholism.

and treatment centers available to help both the alcoholic and the alcoholic's family.

Admitting Addiction and Getting Help

When it comes to facing alcoholism and other forms of substance addiction, talking about it is one thing, but doing something about it is quite another. It is very difficult to say the words, "I am an alcoholic." However it is even more difficult to take the steps necessary to regain physical and emotional health. Some alcoholics are able to voluntarily commit to a recovery program and stick with it. One of these programs is a self-help support group called Alcoholics Anonymous (AA). AA is a nondenominational worldwide network made up of groups of people who meet to share their experiences with one another and help each other build the strengths they need to stop drinking and stay sober. AA is free and runs solely on private donations. The only requirement for membership is a genuine desire to stop drinking. AA does not keep membership records, and a person's participation in the meetings will not be disclosed to anyone. The organization does not make any types of diagnoses or provide treatment facilities, housing, jobs, or money. What it does provide is meetings where alcoholics can talk to others with drinking problems and reinforce their commitment not to drink, a commitment recovering alcoholics live one day at a time. AA also provides sponsors, who are recovering alcoholics who understand the issues newly sober people face on a daily basis.

AA is a twelve-step program. These steps are goals that must be achieved in a particular order. Some of these steps are more difficult for AA members to face than others. First, the alcoholic must admit to being powerless over alcohol. Next the alcoholic must believe that a higher power can restore sanity. The alcoholic must then make the decision to turn his or her life over to some higher power. Following this step, the alcoholic must take a personal, moral inventory of shortcomings and confess these shortcomings to his or her higher power. The alcoholic must then be willing to allow the higher power to remove these character defects. After these personal commitments, the alcoholic must list all of the people he or she harmed by drinking and work to make amends to the individuals the alcoholic has harmed in any way. The alcoholic must maintain a personal inventory of shortcomings and weaknesses and work toward self-improvement through prayer and meditation. Through these steps, the alcoholic should achieve a state of spiritual awakening and make a commitment to share his spiritual journey to sobriety with others.

Addicts Victorious is another faith-based self-help organization. Like AA, Addicts Victorious offers support groups. Unlike AA, though, proponents of Addicts Victorious believe that alcoholics and other addicts can get the help they need and achieve sobriety through five-day Biblical counseling sessions, rather than long-term support meetings. Also, its programs and support groups operate in just a few states, including Texas and Illinois, unlike AA, which is a worldwide organization.

All support groups do not operate on a spiritual theme, though. Groups that are not faith-based are called secular support groups. One of these is Women for Sobriety (WFS), which is headquartered in Pennsylvania. As the name indicates, WFS is a self-help group for female alcoholics. Its New Life Acceptance Program includes thirteen basic statements based on self-empowerment. Among these self-affirming statements are: I have a life-threatening problem that once had me; Negative thoughts destroy only myself; Problems bother me only to the degree I permit them to; I am a competent woman and have much to give life; and I am responsible for myself and my actions.

Another secular self-help group is Save Our Selves (SOS). Like WFS, SOS follows a self-empowerment approach to recovery. Like AA, SOS welcomes all who seek sobriety, offers the support of recovering alcoholics and addicts, and protects the anonymity of the individual. The tenants followed by SOS include overcoming denial, not using insecurities or challenges as excuses to drink, and accepting the fact that alcoholics and drug addicts cannot ever drink or use drugs. Finally, and what appears to be the underlying theme of the SOS recovery program, is that the recovering alcoholic needs to accept the fact that the key to a clean life (being drug or alcohol free), is accepting personal responsibility for sobriety.

Intervention and Residential Treatment

While some alcoholics can regain control over their drinking and other self-destructive behavior solely through the help of support groups, others, especially those with advanced alcoholism, require more radical measures. People suffering from advanced alcoholism sometimes suffer convulsions, hallucinations, mental confusion, and other problems. If the alcoholic reaches a state of behavior like violence or wild hallucinations, which could cause him to harm himself or others, it is time to call for emergency intervention. It may first be necessary to remove family members to a place of safety, such as the home of a friend, neighbor, or other family member, then call for help. Both adults and children are permitted to phone 911 in an emergency. When making a 911 call, it is important to remain as calm as possible and to supply the dispatcher with all necessary information. Police officers will quickly arrive at the site and will take every possible measure to subdue the person safely. If officers observe an immediate threat, one of two things may happen. If the officers determine that the person is violently drunk, he will be taken to jail. However, if the person is hallucinating or exhibiting other symptoms of mental problems, the officers will call for a supervisor who has the authority to issue a document called a mental health warrant. This document permits the person to be secured in a psychiatric ward for 24 hours for evaluation purposes. From this point, the person may be recommended for residential treatment.

Alcoholics with symptoms as serious as these require constant supervision. One way to get help is in a secure, specialized setting, such as a residential treatment center. In a medically supervised treatment center, a patient can be carefully monitored throughout detoxification, often called detox, and successive stages of recovery.

This process begins with a thorough physical examination. In many cases, the patient will be treated with a short-term course of tranquilizers, be placed on bed rest, and be provided specialized nursing care and a carefully balanced diet, because a person in the advanced stages of alcoholism often suffers from malnutrition. When the patient's health is stabilized, he progresses to the rehabilitation phase of treatment. Rehabilitation can occur in the treatment facility or on an outpatient basis, depending on the person's overall physical and psychological condition. This phase includes a moderate exercise program, nutrition therapy, and introduction to a self-help group, such as AA. The final stage of the recovery process is full independence. The patient's progress is monitored through medical and psychological follow-up visits, and he continues to participate in a self-help group.

Residential treatment programs are not without problems, however. The alcoholic may not cooperate with the program, choosing to try to sidestep rules and procedures. People who work in treatment facilities are aware of the many ways patients try to beat the system. Because of their specialized training, they can anticipate many of these attempts and stop them. Failing with the staff, alcoholics will try to get their family members to do something for them that is against the rules or get them to bring things from the outside that are forbidden. Alcoholics are used to manipulating friends and family members, and they may try to continue this behavior even while in the facility, but it is just as important for family members and friends to follow the rules as it is for the person in treatment.

A mother, describing experiences with her daughter, an alcoholic and drug user who was undergoing residential treatment, said,

> She tried to manipulate us in treatment to bring in things that were not allowed like candy and cigarettes and letters from drug using friends, but we told her in advance that we knew the rules and we weren't going to help her break them. She tested us so many times until she learned that she was responsible for her behavior. We had to keep reminding her of the rules and her consequences.[19]

Support for Families

For their own physical and mental welfare, family members of alcoholics need help and support just as much as the person who is undergoing treatment. There are almost as many support groups and agencies for family members and friends as there are for alcoholics. Two of these groups are Al-Anon and Alateen. Al-Anon and Alateen have been providing help for families of alcoholics for over fifty years. Today, there are more than 26,000 Al-Anon and Alateen groups, with chapters in about 115 countries. These groups focus specifically on the welfare and the needs of those closest to alcoholics.

Usually, family members have been in a state of stress, desperation, and helplessness for years before they seek help for themselves. Many have reached the point that they do not believe their family situation will ever improve. They have learned that nagging, preaching, and lecturing do not keep the person from drinking. In fact, the alcoholic will often turn any of these efforts into an excuse to drink more. Although loved ones realize that other families of alcoholics go through bad times, they often feel isolated from the rest of society. At Al-Anon meetings, family members have the opportunity to share their experiences with other families who are dealing with alcoholism. They also learn coping strategies to help them build and improve their own lives, whether the alcoholic family member chose sobriety or not. Local family meeting locations can be found through the Internet, the telephone directory, or by calling 1-888-4AL-ANON (1-888-425-2666). Al-Anon works cooperatively with both health care professionals and law enforcement agencies for the welfare of family members.

Like AA, Al-Anon is a faith-based organization, urging members to submit to a higher power as they perceive it, rather than following any particular religious doctrine. It follows a twelve-step recovery program and operates according to what the organization refers to as twelve traditions. Some of these traditions are: Common welfare (family) comes first; God is the group's authority; Membership-family may include family members, close friends, employers, and co-workers of the alcoholic; The single purpose of Al-Anon is to help family members of alcoholics; and Anonymity is the basis of all of the Al-Anon traditions.

Also like AA, Al-Anon is a long-term association. Family members can attend meetings for weeks, months, or years; however long they feel the need. A parent of an alcoholic teen said of her experiences as a member of Al-Anon,

I have been going to Al-Anon meetings for a number of years since our addicted child went to treatment, and it's amazing to me how much I have to continue to pay attention to the First Step. Some days I am really strong, but on others I slip and my old controlling comes back. In living my program, I challenge myself to be humble and to admit that I need to revisit all the steps. I do so, and

I really appreciate the structure they offer me. It's like I need to look at the map again and retrace my path. Then I get back on the road I want to be on.[20]

In addition to family-based recovery groups, there are also self-help groups for specific family members, such as teenagers. One of these groups is Alateen. Alateen is a special support group that addresses the specific needs of young people. Most Alateen members are between 12 and 18, but some younger children belong as well. In Alateen, young people learn how to emotionally separate the issue of alcohol abuse from the person, so they can continue to love and care about the alcoholic family member. They learn that they are not to blame, they did not cause the person's drinking problem, and they can control only their own behavior—not the behavior of others. They come to accept that they have both the spiritual and the intellectual means to become whatever they want to be, regardless of what is going on at home. They can build successful, rewarding lives for themselves.

As with AA and Al-Anon, Alateen meetings are totally confidential. Names of members are not shared with any other groups or agencies. The privacy of all members is respected and protected, so young people can attend these groups without fear of any repercussions, such as from alcoholic parents who might be angry because they think their children are turning away from them.

Road to Recovery

As discussed earlier, the return to sobriety is not a smooth, hurdle-free process. Backsliding into old habits can occur, which can be tremendously discouraging. Family, friends, and coworkers may have reached the point that they no longer trust the alcoholic's intentions. This is based on their past experiences with the alcoholic. For instance, if the alcoholic person had once talked a family member into co-signing on a loan, with promises that the money, the automobile, or whatever, would be the key to getting his life together, and then the alcoholic fell

Many school systems have programs to help young people learn about the dangers of alcohol abuse.

back into bad habits and lost the ability to repay the loan, the financial burden would have become the responsibility of the co-signer. It would be very difficult for that person to forgive and forget such a hardship. Additionally, some alcoholics have pawned family jewelry, taken household money designated for rent or utilities, and even taken children's personal savings in order to buy more alcohol. They may have hurt family and friends in other ways as well, such as missing graduation ceremonies and other important events in their loved ones' lives, or even worse, showing up at the event drunk. Betrayals like these are very hard to forgive.

In addition to regaining health and sobriety, the alcoholic also has the responsibility of re-earning the trust and respect of the people who have been hurt along the way. Said one 54-year-old recovering alcoholic, ". . . I was allowed to get away with

Online Support

Before the Internet and personal computers, alcoholics and their families had two ways to stay in touch with support groups or sponsors: the telephone and physically attending meetings. Now, though, the Internet has opened other opportunities for support for alcoholics and others with substance abuse issues. Some areas are physically isolated and some communities have no support groups. For people living in such areas, the Internet can be a lifeline that provides a variety of useful support options. Among these are interactive online support groups, bulletin boards, newsgroups, and chat rooms. Many are sponsored by well-known groups such as Alcoholics Anonymous, Al-Anon, and Alateen.

things for a long time but gradually people drop you because you say and do stupid things. Now I am working on my own. I'm doing well and gradually regaining trust, but it is taking some time."[21]

What many recovering alcoholics learn is that sometimes regaining self-respect and trust is a harder and longer process than learning to stay away from alcohol. However, alcoholics who are truly committed to improving their lives, regaining control over their behavior, and re-establishing healthy relationships will find the results are worth the work.

Education

The best way to maintain a healthy lifestyle is to not fall into the alcohol abuse cycle in the first place. Today, many school systems, colleges, and universities have a curriculum in place to help students make healthy lifestyle choices. On the elementary school level, children in the first and second grades are taught to identify the difference between harmful and non-harmful substances. Alcohol is considered a harmful substance, one not to be touched by children. Students learn to report harmful substances to adults, so they may be put out of the way of younger siblings. In seventh and eighth grades, students learn about support groups and community organizations that help families deal with substance abuse. These older students are taught how to use safe decision-making and problem-solving skills and ways to refuse harmful substances without getting into conflicts. They also learn about negative consequences that result from substance abuse and positive ways to relieve stress without having to resort to drugs or alcohol. In high school, students learn about alcohol abuse and addiction, the physical, social, and emotional consequences of alcoholism, and responses to peer pressure.

Additionally, many colleges and universities nationwide are working to change so-called traditions on their own campuses that appear to promote out-of-control drinking. In addition to distributing pamphlets to new students, many campuses now have mandatory alcohol awareness classes for transferring or freshman students. At Michigan Tech, for instance, Vice Provost for Student Affairs Martha Janners said,

> Educating students about the norm when it comes to drug and alcohol abuse is our goal. When many students come to college, they assume that everyone is abusing alcohol, so they do the same. Our job is to redefine what students assume to be normal behavior, and we feel peer educators are instrumental in such an effort.[22]

Besides providing alcohol-alternative social activities for students, Boston College also has a comprehensive educational program for their campus, which includes alcohol and drug education classes for students, alcohol and drug abuse training for faculty and staff, and alcoholism resources materials for the surrounding community.

The Massachusetts Institute of Technology (MIT) goes beyond educating students regarding alcohol abuse. MIT is also involved in alcohol and drug education programs for employees. Faculty advisers, housemasters, resident tutors, resident assistants, and chaplains are all trained to spot potential alcohol and drug abuse problems among students so that steps can be quickly taken to get them the help they need. Also, individual students as well as student organizations receive training regarding the social, academic, personal, and legal consequences resulting from any type of substance abuse.

Regardless of the efforts made by schools, colleges, communities, and health agencies, the best defense against alcohol abuse and alcoholism is a personal sense of responsibility. People have to make their own choices. Individuals have to make the decision to learn how to distance themselves from unhealthy situations; seek professional help if they have already slipped into an out-of-control relationship with alcohol; and once admitting the problem, be willing to do the work and invest the time in regaining their health, self respect, and the respect of friends and family.

Notes

Introduction: Alcoholism: Compulsive Behavior or Disease?
1. Quoted in Harvey Haisong, *Alcohol*. Farmington Hills, MI: Greenhaven, 2003. p.14.
2. Quoted in Eric Newhouse, *Alcohol: Cradle to Grave*. Center City, MN: Hazelden, 2001. p. 24.

Chapter 1: How Serious a Problem is Alcoholism?
3. Quoted in James Torr, ED, *Teens and Alcohol*. Farmington Hills, MI: Greenhaven, 2001. p.14.
4. Quoted in Power Hour VX. www.powerhourvx_drinking_game_beer_quotes_alcohol_quotes.htm.
5. Quoted in Power Hour VX.
6. Quoted in Power Hour VX.
7. Quoted in Power Hour VX.
8. Quoted in Power Hour VX.
9. Quoted in Judy Monroe, *Alcohol*. Berkley Heights, NJ: Enslow Publishers. 1994. p. 42.

Chapter 2: Dangers of Alcohol and Alcoholism
10. Quoted in Effects of Alcohol. www.faadrug.com/alcohol.asp.
11. Quoted in Newhouse, *Alcohol: Cradle to Grave*. p.57.

Chapter 3: Alcoholism and the Family
12. From author interview. Name withheld by request.
13. From author interview. Name withheld by request.

Chapter 4: Alcoholism and Peer Pressure

14. Quoted in Smokers' Club, Inc. www.smokersclubinc.com/modules.php?name=news&file=article&sid=4204.
15. Quoted in Lowe Family Foundation for Families Coping with Alcoholism. www.lowefamily.org/interviews/jan99_Alcoholism.
16. Quoted in Henry Wechsler, PhD and Bernice Wuethrich, *Dying to Drink: Confronting Binge Drinking on College Campuses*. Emmaus, PA: St. Martin's, 2002. p.12.
17. Quoted in Nikki Babbit, *Adolescent Drug and Alcohol Abuse: How to Spot It, Stop It, and Get Help for Your Family*. Sebastapool, CA: O'Rielly and Associates, 2000. p. 44.

Chapter 5: Roads to Recovery and the Power of Knowledge

18. Quoted in About Alcoholism and Substance Abuse: Making Healthy Choices. www.Alcoholism.about.com/cs/relapse/a/aa000201a.htm.
19. Quoted in Babbit, *Adolescent Drug and Alcohol Abuse*, p. 207.
20. Quoted in Babbit, *Adolescent Drug and Alcohol Abuse*, p. 221.
21. Quoted in BBC News UK Personal Cost of Liquid Lunches. www.news.bbc.co.uk/1/hi/uk/2785711.stm.
22. Quoted in Michigan Tech, "Janners Addresses MTU's Steps Toward Substance Abuse Prevention." www.admin.mtu.edu/rel/breaking2000/substance.html.

Glossary

abstinence: Restraining from indulging in substances such as alcohol.

acetaldehyde: A colorless, flammable liquid used in the manufacture of perfumes and certain drugs.

ADD: Attention Deficit Disorder is a pattern of impulsive behavior, short attention span, and often hyperactivity.

AIDS: Acquired Immune Deficiency Syndrome is a contagious disease that greatly weakens the immune system. It is transmitted through blood and body fluids.

Al-Anon: A self-help group for families and friends of alcoholics.

Alateen: A self-help group for teen family members of alcoholics.

alcohol dependence: A physical or psychological dependence on alcoholic beverages.

alcoholic hepatitis: An inflammatory liver disease usually associated with long-term and excessive consumption of alcohol.

alcohol poisoning: The serious and often deadly result of absorbing too much alcohol into the body. Characterized by slow breathing and heart rate.

Alcoholics Anonymous: A twelve-step, self-help group for alcoholics who are seeking to recover sobriety.

alcoholism: A chronic condition caused by dependence on alcohol.

carcinogen: A cancer-causing substance.

cirrhosis: A chronic liver disease, usually caused by alcoholism, characterized by loss of functional liver cells.

cocktail: An alcoholic mixed drink, usually chilled and sweetened.

compulsive behavior: A condition in which a person consumes a substance, such as alcohol, compulsively; apparently with no self-control.

congestive heart failure: A cardiac disorder that affects the heart's ability to fill with or pump a sufficient amount of blood.

dehydration: The body's loss of water. In extreme cases, this can lead to mental confusion and even coma.

delirium tremens: Periods of hallucination often associated with substance withdrawal. Also called DTs.

demographic: A portion of the population.

depressant: A substance that depresses the nervous system.

diuretic: A drug used to increase urine output.

dopamine: A chemical compound found in the brain and the peripheral nervous system.

Dry Law: Also called Prohibition, a law that prevents the manufacturing, import, export, or sale of alcoholic beverages.

euphoria: A state of intense happiness, sometimes associated with excessive drug or alcohol consumption.

fatty liver: A condition wherein fat accumulates in liver cells.

fetus: Unborn young; still in the womb.

gaba: A neurotransmitter of the central nervous system.

gastritis: The inflammation of mucous membranes of the stomach.

genetics: The science of heredity.

hangover: The after effects of excessive drinking, which may include headache, nausea, vomiting, and diarrhea.

hemorrhage: Profuse bleeding.

histamines: Substances found in plant and animal tissue that can cause allergic reactions, such as itching and sneezing.

HIV: A retrovirus that causes AIDS.

incest: Sexual relations between closely related people.

intoxication: Drunkenness.

malnutrition: A condition caused by poor diet.

metabolize: To undergo a change.

National Survey on Drug Use and Health: Sponsored by the Substance Abuse and Mental Health Services Administration, an agency of the United States Public Health Service, NSDUH provides annual information on substance abuse in the United States.

Office of National Drug Control Policy: A governmental agency that establishes policies and objectives regarding United States drug control programs.

polyamines: A type of organic compound.

Prohibition: Legally preventing the import, export, manufacture, and sale of alcoholic beverages.

serotonin: A neurotransmitter involved in neurological processes such as memory, sleep, and depression.

speakeasies: Nightclubs or saloons where alcoholic beverages were sold illegally.

stroke: The loss of consciousness due to rupture of blood vessels, depriving the brain of oxygen.

Wernicke-Korsakoff's Psychosis: A brain disorder involving loss of certain brain functions. This condition can be brought on by alcoholism.

Organizations to Contact

Addicts Victorious

639 York St. Suite 210, Quincy, IL 622301
(800) 323-1388
e-mail: victory@addictsvictorious.com
www.addictsvictorious.com

This faith-based organization has group meeting sites in Illinois, Iowa, Missouri, and Texas. Additionally, Addicts Victorious offers five-day Biblical counseling sessions aimed at delivering alcoholics and other addicts from substance abuse.

Al-Anon

1600 Corporate Landing Parkway, Virginia Beach,
VA 2354-5617
(888) 425-2666
e-mail: wso@al-anon.org
www.al-anon.org

Aligned with Alcoholics Anonymous, Al-Anon focuses on the welfare and recovery of the friends and family members of the alcoholic, rather than the alcoholic, through group meetings and shared experiences. Members' privacy is protected.

Alateen

1600 Corporate Landing Parkway, Virginia Beach,
VA 2354-5617
(888) 425-2666
e-mail: wso@al-anon.org
www.al-anon.alateen.org

With ties to Al-Anon and Alcoholics Anonymous, this organization focuses on the welfare and recovery of teen family members, rather than the alcoholic. Teens in groups share their experiences and challenges. Member privacy is protected.

Alcoholics Anonymous

AA World Services, Inc., PO Box 459, New York, NY 10163
(888) 425-2666
www.alcoholics-anonymous.org

A twelve-step, spirit-based recovery organization with worldwide membership that encourages alcoholics to admit their powerlessness over alcohol and to surrender their will to a higher power on their path to recovery. AA is supported through private donations rather than membership dues. Members' names are not shared with the media or any other organization.

Save Our Selves

4773 Hollywood Blvd., Hollywood, CA 90027
(323) 666-4295
e-mail: sos@secularsobriety.org
www.secularsobriety.org

With membership in the United States and other countries, this abstinence based, self-empowerment organization maintains the anonymity of its participants. Their goal is to achieve and maintain sobriety through personal responsibility and self-reliance. Supported through private donations, rather than dues.

SMART Recovery

7537 Mentor Ave., Suite 306, Mentor, OH 44060
(866) 951-5357
e-mail: info@smartrecovery.org
www.smartrecovery.org

In addition to providing more than three hundred face-to-face groups worldwide, this organization provides both online support groups and a message board. Based on a four-part recovery program, SMART Recovery does not charge membership dues. It is supported through private donations.

Women for Sobriety

PO Box 618, Quakertown, PA 18951-0618
(215) 536-8026
e-mail:NewLife@nni.com
www.womenforsobriety.org

This self-help program for female alcoholics is based on the recovery needs of women. This organization can be used alone or in conjunction with other groups and is supported through donations. Membership is anonymous.

For Further Reading

Books

Nikki Babbit, *Adolescent Drug and Alcohol Abuse: How to Spot It, Stop It, and Get Help for Your Family.* Sebastapool, CA: O'Reilly and Associates, 2000. Written by the child of substance-dependent parents, this book discusses issues such as communication, relationships, treatments, and rehabilitation.

Kenneth Blum, PhD, in collaboration with James E. Payne, *Alcohol and the Addictive Brain.* New York: The Free Press, 1991. This book includes the stigma of alcoholism, physiology of alcohol's effects on the body, and approaches to treatment.

Griffith Edwards, *Alcohol: The World's Favorite Drug.* New York: St. Martin's, 2000. Provides a history of drunkenness, myths about alcohol and alcohol consumption, and research on alcoholism.

Harvey Haisong, *Alcohol Abuse.* San Diego, CA: Greenhaven, 2003. An anthology of articles debating such issues as whether alcoholism is or is not a disease, treatment programs, and actions colleges should promote regarding alcohol consumption.

Judy Monroe, *Alcohol.* Berkley Heights, NJ: Enslow Publishers, 1994. Describes the effects of alcohol, identifies alcoholism in demographic groups, and provides information regarding legal intoxication and the DWI arrest procedure.

James D. Toor, Ed, *Alcoholism.* San Diego, CA: Greenhaven, 2000. Includes articles debating whether alcoholism is a disease or a behavior, the effectiveness of certain well-known treatment programs, and the issue of government regulation.

Websites

Al-Anon (www.al-anon) This Web site provides help and direction for family members of alcoholics.

Alateen (www.al-anon.alateen.org) This Web site is specifically dedicated to the needs of teen members of the alcoholic family.

The Cool Spot (www.thecoolspot.gov) A Web site about alcohol and resisting peer pressure, this site is specifically designed for older children and teens.

Fact Sheets and Pamphlets

National Institute on Alcohol Abuse and Alcoholism

–New Years, Old Myths, New Fatalities,
December, 2006.

–Parents: Help Your Teens Party Right at Graduation,
May 2005.

–A Family History of Alcoholism: Are You at Risk?
August 2005.

–Alcohol: A Woman's Health Issue,
August 2003.

–Age Page: Alcohol Use and Abuse,
September 2002.

Index

Abdominal pains, 12
Absenteeism, 51
Abstinence method, of
  treatment, 12
Accidents, alcoholism and,
  44–46, 48–51
  drunk driving, 44, 45, 46, 48
  falls/tripping, 44, 45, 48, 50
  fires, at home, 48
  home accidents, 50
Acetaldehyde, 43
Addiction to alcohol, 14–15,
  17–24
Admission of alcoholism,
  57–58
Adult children of alcoholics,
  64
Advertising, alcohol related,
  24–28
African American couples, 62
AIDS/HIV, 44
Al-Anon support group, 88,
  89–90
Alateen support group, 88, 90
Alcohol
  addictive nature of, 14–15
  behaviors related to, 32–33
  body's reaction to, 36–39
  cholesterol (HDL)
    influenced by, 41
  dangers of, 35–42
  disguising of, with flavors/
    juices, 23–24
  economic aspects of, 11,
    24–25
  influence on unborn

children, 65–67
media promotion of, 24–28
medication interactions
  with, 36, 42
mixing types of, 30
myths about, 28–32
nonthreatening nature of, 16
strategies for reducing
  effect of, 30–31
types of, 35
Alcoholics, 10
  backsliding by, 59
  children of, 11, 54, 55, 60
  cyclical drinking patterns
    of, 53
  desperation of, 35
  family manipulation by, 56
  increased injuries of, 50
Alcoholics Anonymous (AA),
  12, 83
Alcohol industry, ties to
  professional sports, 27–28
Alcoholism
  accidents and, 44–46, 48–51
  advertising and, 24–28
  in colleges, 74–778
  compulsive behavior model
    of, 9–11
  dangers of, 35–42
  denial of, 56, 86
  disease model of, 11–12
  diseases/organ damage
    from, 39–44
  media portrayal of, 23, 24–28
  myths contributing to, 28–32
  peer pressure and, 68–81

Photo Credits

About the Author

A retired teacher, Sheila Wyborny, and her husband, Wendell, a consulting engineer, live in a private airport community near Houston, Texas.